A History of
Leaders in the Making

Published by Looking Glass Books
Decatur, Georgia

Manufactured in Canada
ISBN 1-929619-30-8

Book design by Burtch Hunter Design
Jacket design by brand|apart and Pixel Peach Studio ~ www.pixelpeach.com

A History of
Leaders in the Making

Rick Johnson

Foreword

S. TRUETT CATHY

Commit to the LORD whatever you do, and your plans will succeed.
Proverbs 16:3

Leaders in the making. That's been our vision for WinShape Camps since 1985. That and having fun. It's exciting to see how God works in the lives of children during their two weeks at summer camp. When they're away from their parents, they learn to rely more on Him, seeking Him in prayer and scripture. Campers walk through the woods and the rolling hills of northwest Georgia and see His beautiful creation all around, and the experience deepens their Christian faith and sharpens their character.

On Sunday morning midway through every camp session, I worship with the campers, and we talk about priorities: God comes first, others second, and I am third. That philosophy is the essence of true leadership and the foundation of WinShape Camps.

In this book, WinShape Camps founding director Rick Johnson tells the history of our camp and many of the stories from two decades of camping: more than twenty years of sock wars and "Bobos," rock climbs and council rings. God has blessed us with thousands of campers, and we look forward to thousands more.

Contents

In the Beginning. 1

The Value of Time Shared 9

Camp Ridgecrest "God, Give Me Strength" 13

A Life-Changing Night at Camp 17

First Session 21

Tennis Lesson 27

"I Will Never Leave You" 31

Camp Challenges Reveal Character. 35

Gate of Opportunity 39

Meeting in Truett's Tree House 45

Building a Camp 49

Small Acts of Encouragement. 55

Sock War 59

Trust the Rope. 63

Communicating Love. 67

Speedy. 73

Enduring Eagle 79

The Light of the World. 83

Through Grace, God's Plan Emerges. 87

Janie Bird. 91

A Shared Passion 95

A Tribe of Their Own 99

Alathea: Truth 103

The Great Chippewa Massacre 107

The Language of Forgiveness. 111

On the Mountaintop 117

From Wilderness to Wilderness 121

A Call to Serve 125

Passionate Starlight's First Indian Dance 131

New-Found Leadership 135

Why We Do What We Do 139

A History of
Leaders in the Making

In the Beginning

"For I know the plans I have for you," declares the LORD, "plans to prosper you
and not to harm you, plans to give you hope and a future."

Jeremiah 29:11

God's plans are so great, we usually don't see them until we look back over the course of
time. That's the way it is with Camp WinShape. Looking back we can see that six decades
before the first children arrived at camp in 1985, God was already building WinShape's foun-
dations in hearts and on the land.

Historians often describe the 1920s as the Roaring Twenties, a time when it seemed that
all Americans had good jobs and cash in their pockets. But poverty still held a firm grip on
pockets of the rural South and in some corners of the big cities. In three of those crucibles
of hard times—a boarding house in west Atlanta, the hills of northwest Georgia, and the
mountains of North Carolina—God was at work.

In the late nineteenth century, Martha Berry, daughter of wealthy parents living just north of Rome, Georgia, met some of her poor neighbors. With no public school nearby, the children were receiving no education. Most of the families had only one book in the house, a Bible, but since neither parent could read, it sat unopened. So Miss Berry invited children to a cabin in the woods on Sundays and told them Bible stories. Then she began to teach them to read, and in 1902 she founded a school on Lavender Mountain.

By the 1920s, with the help of generous benefactors and the hard work of Berry School students, the school was moving beyond its log cabin beginnings, and the campus that would become the center of Camp WinShape was built. In 1923 students built Hill Dining Hall with its massive stone fireplace and beamed cathedral ceilings. Two years later students went back to work building Friendship Hall, a stone dormitory with a two-story beamed cathedral ceiling and natural stone fireplace, and the Mountain Campus began to take the look of a New England boarding school in the rural South. Four years later another stone dormitory, Pilgrim Hall, was built by student labor to house sixty-five Berry residents. In 1930 a stone barn was built at the foot of the mountain.

In the meantime, the Great Depression had struck and Martha Berry experienced tremendous difficulty raising money for the school's operations. She spent days and weeks on the road traveling to Washington, New York, and anywhere else she might meet with potential benefactors. She raised enough money to build the Normandy complex during the period from 1931-37. Again students provided labor, this time using bricks and roof tiles they had made in the campus brick plant. The barns housed Berry's dairy operation, where cows were milked twice daily, and the dormitories housed students working in the dairy or on the farm. Miss Berry had the student builders place spires on every barn so that whenever people passed, their eyes would turn to God.

At this point, the key element missing at the Mountain Campus, Miss Berry said, was a suitable chapel. She prayed that God would make the resources available, and then put a little wooden cross on the lawn with the words: CHAPEL WANTED.

Not long afterward she received a letter from a man in Los Angeles who had been reading about the Berry schools. He would be coming south in the spring and would like to see the campus. A few months later Howard Frost and his wife called from Chattanooga, wishing they could visit but understanding that spring floods made the campus nearly inaccessible from the north. Not so, Miss Berry said, and she had a staff member drive the back roads to the Frosts' hotel and bring them back to Rome. As she came to know the Frosts, Miss Berry learned they had lost their only son when he was about the age of her students. They wanted to create an appropriate memorial to him, perhaps a chapel. Martha Berry's heart must have leapt, realizing God's provision seemed so close at hand. But instead of jumping at the opportunity, she quietly suggested that they continue looking over the Mountain Campus. As they passed a long sloping hill, the Frosts said it looked like the ideal spot for the chapel they envisioned. By October of the same year, Frost Chapel was completed and ready for worship.

If the Joseph Benjamin Cathy family had lived seventy miles north of Atlanta, their children might have been prospective students for Martha Berry's schools. Mr. Cathy went broke as a farmer in rural Eatonton, Georgia, and the family moved to Atlanta soon after their seventh child, Samuel Truett, was born. In Atlanta Mr. Cathy began selling life insurance, but still was unable to earn enough money to support the family.

The experience affected Truett Cathy's father deeply. He became stern, sometimes harsh, with his children, and he was rarely if ever loving. Truett never heard his father say, "I love you." And though Truett was well behaved, as you would imagine, he often felt the sting of his father's belt or a razor strap.

Unable to live on Mr. Cathy's income from selling insurance, the Cathys rented a big house and took in boarders for a dollar a day. Mrs. Cathy ran the boarding house. Unlike Mr. Cathy, who was embittered by hard times, his wife, Lilla, remained gentle and loving as she relied more heavily on God to help her family. Running the boarding house was a seven-day-a-week job, including Sunday dinner during the worship hour, but she made sure that her children got dressed and off to Sunday school and church every week. At home she tuned her radio to the Reverend Charles E. Fuller reading the Bible and preaching on "Old Fashioned Revival Hour." That was church for her.

Martha Berry would have appreciated Truett's ambition. Truett turned eight years old in 1929, the year of the stock market crash and the beginning of the Depression. He decided that it was time for him to earn his own money. He started selling Coca-Colas door-to-door, buying a six-pack for a quarter and selling them for a nickel each, giving him a nickel profit. This was no small task for a young boy with a speech impediment so severe he couldn't pronounce his own name. But with determination he succeeded. Four years later he got his first paper route, throwing the Atlanta Journal after school and before daybreak on Sunday mornings.

About the same time, Truett's Sunday school teacher saw this boy growing into a man without a godly male role influence. Theo Abby, who had a son Truett's age, reached out with a loving and caring spirit, visiting the Cathy home and taking Truett and other boys on overnight trips to Lake Jackson. Truett knew then that Theo Abby would become his model as an adult. He would reach out to children whose fathers had neglected them.

While Truett was growing up in Atlanta and Martha Berry was building the Mountain Campus, a summer camp was taking shape in the Blue Ridge Mountains near Asheville, North Carolina. In the mid-1920s, the Southern Baptist Convention Board bought property near its Ridgecrest Baptist Conference Center and built a fifteen-acre lake with the intention of opening a girls' camp on one side of the lake and a boys' camp on the other. A large two-story residence on the property became a camp headquarters building, and several cabins and other facilities were added in time to open for the 1926 camping season. Camp Swannanoa for girls opened, but in 1928 after only three seasons, logistical business issues caused it to close.

The Baptist Sunday School Board took charge in 1929 and focused its efforts on opening a boys' camp. A two-week trial session that summer was deemed a success, and plans began in earnest to open Camp Ridgecrest in 1930.

Asheville and Buncombe County appeared to have everything going their way. Good times led to the building of a new city hall, a sixteen-story county courthouse, and the relocation of a large library. When the stock market crashed, Asheville was left with the highest per capita debt in the nation.

The Sunday School Board refused to allow hard times to impede plans for its summer camp. They moved forward with the same determination that had led to the building of the Conference Center in 1907:

> The men who founded Ridgecrest may have realized the same educational values of the mountains as was reflected in the words of Dr. John A. Broadus when in 1874 he wrote of John the Baptist: "He was a child of the mountains. Whenever education and religion take hold in a mountain region, the result is great strength of character."
>
> — *Ridgecrest: Mountain of Faith*, Kenneth McAnear

A young student at Yale, Charles W. Burts, was selected as camp director, a choice that would have a permanent impact on Ridgecrest and on WinShape half a century later. Burts came to Ridgecrest having worked for five summers as a counselor and an assistant director in other camps. He and Noble Van Ness, who was leading the camp effort for the Sunday School Board and was an experienced Boy Scout leader, decided to build a program around a Native American motif. In the summer of 1930, campers and staff at Ridgecrest divided into tribes according to age and met around the Council Ring for the first time.

The camp leaders believed children would be more likely to succeed in camp if they were recognized for their achievements. They created a system of ranks that boys could earn culminating in the highest honor, Little Chief, which was to be earned only by the most outstanding campers following an overnight ordeal. That ordeal was patterned in part on the Boy Scout honor society, Order of the Arrow. During the Little Chief test, candidates had to maintain complete silence while working to keep a fire burning through the night. Then at daybreak they climbed to the top of a nearby mountain where they listened to a morning devotional, then wrote an essay about the value of their camp experience and worked all day on camp improvement projects.

The camp program at Ridgecrest offered a variety of activities, all with a strong Christian emphasis that was built into every aspect of camp life. Every day, campers gathered for morning watch and evening devotions.

Independent of one another, the Berry schools, Truett Cathy, Camp Ridgecrest, and the girls' camp that followed later, Camp Crestridge, would glorify God while having a positive influence on literally thousands of young people. Then in 1985, God would bring these pillars together and build upon them Camp WinShape, a place for strengthening character and shaping winners.

The Value of Time Shared

At the age of twelve, I learned that I wasn't the athlete I thought I was. I didn't take the news well, but the lesson stayed with me for the rest of my life.

My parents had sent me to a week-long sports camp that summer, and I took the opportunity to follow in my father's footsteps to become a baseball pitcher. Little League coaches back home had never given me a chance to pitch, but I knew it was in my blood. I could throw strikes and get batters out.

All week I told my counselor that I could pitch—that I had pitched—and all week he kept putting me in the outfield. Finally, it was the last game of camp, and I knew that if I went back home without pitching in this game, I might never get another opportunity. I turned up the pressure in the dugout and convinced my counselor that I could get these guys out if he would just give me a chance.

He did, and I was thrilled. I was finally standing where I belonged, where I had fantasized standing for years, up on the mound, right toe on the rubber, staring down at the catcher's mitt. I threw some warm-up pitches and felt good. I was keeping the ball close to the plate with good velocity. The first batter stepped into the box, and the umpire yelled, "Play ball!" I took a deep breath to calm myself, then I wound up and threw my first pitch a foot outside. The catcher threw the ball back, and I wound up again. This time I hit the batter in the leg. He trotted off to first base, and another batter stepped in.

Never having pitched in a game, I had no mental routine for throwing strikes. I decided to focus on the mitt instead of the batter, and I threw a perfect strike. The batter ripped it into centerfield. One by one they came to the plate, and I either hit them or walked them, or if I got the ball over the plate, they crushed it.

I stomped around the mound in frustration and embarrassment, wondering when my counselor would come and take me out of the game. The other team had batted around when he finally came out and asked, "Had enough?"

I didn't answer. I just gave him the ball and stomped off the field.

That night we all went to supper, and everybody else had forgotten about the game. They were laughing and having a good time. Not me. I was wallowing in my humiliation, and refused to speak to anybody.

The next morning my counselor asked me to go with him for a canoe ride during free time. "Sure," I said, and I couldn't wait to show him how well I could paddle, even though I had never been in a canoe. We glided out to the middle of the lake with him at the stern, then he laid his paddle in the canoe. I turned around to see why he had stopped. I expected he was going to lecture me about the game. He didn't. Instead, he built me up, talking about the things I did well. Then he talked about how I could improve my attitude and behavior. I had never had anybody talk to me about those things.

I don't remember all the things he said that day, but I'll never forget the feeling, as we paddled back to shore, that he had given up his free time to spend time with me. He wasn't just doing his job. He really cared.

That was more than fifty years ago, but the impact of my counselor's caring affects everything we do at Camp WinShape.

Camp Ridgecrest
"God, Give Me Strength"

I arrived at Camp Ridgecrest in the summer of 1961 as a nineteen-year-old rising sophomore in college to serve as a camp counselor. I had never done anything like this before, but I thought the work would suit my skills and interests. I loved sports, especially basketball, and I enjoyed working with young people. I had coached a basketball team of ten- to twelve-year-old boys at our little Baptist church in Oxford, Alabama. I also had a semester of college psychology under my belt. With all those skills and experiences under my belt, I knew I was ready to go, right? Wrong.

First, I didn't think I would ever get there. I rode the bus from Oxford to Asheville, and the three-hundred-mile trip took twelve hours. I had never seen mountains as beautiful as those in western North Carolina, and I had never ridden on roads with so many curves around the mountains. Back and forth we would go up the narrow road to the top of one mountain, then back and forth down the back side. By the time we reached Asheville, I felt like I had ridden across the country.

I was met at the station by the director of Camp Ridgecrest, Wayne Chastain, and a couple of returning counselors, Jerald Ellington and Gilbert Luttrell. I put my bag in the station wagon and we headed over to the train station to pick up another counselor coming up from New Orleans. Along the way I learned that Jerald and Gilbert were All-America basketball players from Carson-Newman College, a small-college basketball power at the time. The guy we were going to pick up was Ronnie Santamount, an outstanding football player at a junior college in southern Louisiana. I was beginning to think this was going to be a fun summer. I had always wanted to work at a sports camp.

As we rode to the train station, Wayne, Jerald, and Gilbert told me about the competitive basketball league I was about to become a part of. The Camp Ridgecrest staff played in a well-organized, highly competitive athletic association among summer camp and retreat staffs in the area. The counselors competed in basketball, fast-pitch softball, volleyball, track, and swimming. In fact, our first basketball game was just a week away. Those of us who were athletes were being brought in a week early to train and practice for the summer staff basketball season. We had a two-week staff training-period plan—first a week of grueling basketball practice, then an equally challenging week for the entire camp staff to prepare for the arrival of campers.

Before we reached the train station, I learned just how competitive the basketball games were going to be. Camp Rockmont had several players from Mississippi State University, which had won the Southeastern Conference championship. Montreat Conference had some local junior college players. Mishemokwa, a basketball camp in the area, had most of Auburn's starters, and the Blue Ridge Assembly had a couple of starters from Wake Forest's Atlantic Coast Conference championship team.

We arrived at the train station to pick up Ronnie, who was wearing a coat and tie and carrying two huge footlockers like they were overnight bags. Underneath that coat, I knew he must be hard as a rock. He put the footlockers down and extended his hand. His grip nearly squashed my hand, but I didn't let on. Wayne asked Jerald and me to put Ronnie's footlockers in the car. Jerald picked up one of them, but I couldn't budge the other. I had to get Gilbert to help me. Before that day I would have told you that I was a stronger-than-average nineteen year old, that I was a decent basketball player, and that I could hold my own in a crowd of college men. Along the eighteen-mile drive through the dark to camp, I began to question that assessment. I learned that Ronnie's footlockers were filled with four hundred pounds of weights he planned to use all summer to stay in shape.

It was nearly nine o'clock now, and the North Carolina night had turned black as a Bible. The mountains seemed higher and the curves sharper than any I had seen earlier in the day. Then I saw the Camp Ridgecrest sign and the words: "GOD, GIVE ME MOUNTAINS TO CLIMB AND THE STRENGTH TO CLIMB THEM." Somewhere deep inside, I began to realize that real strength would not come from lifting weights or winning on the basketball court. My strength would come from God.

A Life-Changing Night at Camp

The night I arrived at Camp Ridgecrest, I had no time to unpack and put away my clothes. "Get into your basketball shorts and shoes and hit the floor in fifteen minutes!" Wayne Chastain called. I followed Jerald and Gilbert, running to keep up, to the cabin where we would be staying for the first week of training. Then we hustled over to the gym, which was like nothing I had ever seen—the tallest log structure in the world. On each side were screened-in dining halls and in the middle was the basketball court, a little smaller than regulation. At one end of the court was a huge stone fireplace covered with wrestling mats so we wouldn't crash into it going for a rebound. Two feet beyond the other end line was a log wall with another wrestling mat hanging on it. The backboards were wood, and the rims were thick and black.

Wayne was standing in the middle of the court looking more like a coach than a camp director. In fact, he wore a T-shirt with "COACH" written across the chest. I looked around at the other nine guys and felt skinny and weak. I weighed about 160 pounds with arms and legs like sticks. I didn't remember looking so undernourished with my high school team, but I realized that I was entering a level of competition I had never known. Jerald stood six-feet-four and looked like a buffalo. Gilbert was only about five-feet-ten, but he was muscular and athletic looking. Everybody else was six-feet-four or taller and looking lean and mean.

Wayne divided us into teams, and Jerald guarded me. The two tallest guys stood for the tipoff, and before Wayne tossed the ball up he said, "All right, let's see what we've got this summer." The ball went up and it was tipped straight to me. Jerald knocked it out of my hands and flipped it out to Gilbert, who raced down the floor for a layup.

The whole scrimmage went like that. I was embarrassed from the beginning and mortified by the end. This was going to be a long summer.

After the scrimmage Wayne told us we could take one of the camp station wagons into town to get something to eat. I was surprised when the guys invited me to come along. After my showing in the scrimmage, I figured they would be leaving me behind. I showered and dressed, and Jerald told me to grab my Bible and come over to his cabin for a group Bible study before we went into town. This was new to me. I had never been involved in anything like that. I wasn't even sure what he meant by "group Bible study."

I had grown up in a church and was a regular at Sunday school, but outside of church the adults took us to ballgames and fishing trips more often than they led us in Bible study. I had certainly never been in a Bible study led by someone my age.

Nine of us arrived at Jerald's cabin about the same time. He opened his Bible and read something about how important it was that we really knew that Christ was in our heart, because once the campers arrived, our focus would shift from basketball to the kids. We had to be ready to counsel them and model Christ in everything we did. Then Jerald prayed, but he didn't say "amen." The guy beside him prayed, and when he finished the next guy prayed. Everybody was going to pray, and they were all doing it as easily as they had been playing basketball a few minutes earlier. My turn was coming, and I started feeling inadequate again. I stumbled through a few words—I don't remember what I said. But just like on the basketball court, at least nobody laughed at me. Jerald closed the prayer and we all loaded into the station wagon and drove off into the late night for a hamburger.

I didn't say much as we drove toward Asheville. Instead I pondered all the things I had experienced in the last couple of hours. I had learned that good athletes could be sincere Christians. I learned that you could play hard, knock everybody around, and physically run over somebody in a game in the spirit of good sportsmanship, and afterward bring everybody back together in Christian fellowship. I learned that if you truly have Christ in your heart, you can be comfortable with yourself and have no problem sharing Him with someone else.

Sometime later in the summer I looked back and realized it was on that night I became a Christian. I had already been baptized, but the experience hadn't really sunk in that knowing Christ and accepting his Son was what it was all about. That night I came to know what it meant. You can be a man and a believer at the same time.

Since that night I have spent every summer of my life trying to create an atmosphere where everyone—campers and staff—can feel free to come to a special place where God can be shared comfortably and His Spirit demonstrated on a daily basis; a place where everyone, counselors, instructors, or maintenance staff members, exhibits the spirit of Christ.

First Session

Eight of the nine boys and the junior counselor in my first cabin had been coming to Ridgecrest for years. At the age of twelve, several of the boys already talked about going into the ministry after college or becoming coaches or teachers. I had more potential in my cabin than any other cabin in camp, and I felt responsible for getting the most out of them. I was going to mold them into men.

The best way I knew to do that was to follow the model of Gilbert Adams, my high school football and basketball coach. Through discipline he had built us into strong individuals and a strong team. We spent hours, it seemed, working on passing a basketball to the other guy's outside shoulder.

I started my guys at camp with the little things. Boys from other cabins walked in groups to the mess hall for meals, talking the whole way. I had my guys line up and walk like men, single file, eyes straight ahead. At night, lights out at ten meant lights out at ten, and not a minute later. When a boy didn't toe the line, he stepped aside and gave me some push-ups or ran a lap to remind him to do better next time. By the end of the first week, I was whipping them into shape. I didn't enjoy it, but I knew it was for the best.

Two boys required more attention than the others. Both were twelve years old, but Richard looked like he was about eight, skinny and baby faced, and Carl looked sixteen. Carl played football back home, and in one of his two footlockers he had brought weights to work out with all summer. Richard was a bookworm, really intelligent, and Carl was a bully, constantly needling and pushing Richard—shoving too hard whenever he got a chance in a game. Richard got even with his wit, making Carl the object of his jokes or sarcasm.

The only thing Richard and Carl agreed on was how much they disliked me. In fact, none of the boys liked me, as it turned out. They had been coming to camp for years to have fun, and my discipline was turning it into drudgery.

I ran back to the cabin one night in the rain and hit the door. It didn't budge, so I pushed harder. Still it didn't open, so I rammed it with my shoulder. Finally the door flew open and stuff came piling down on top of me. My campers had booby-trapped the door. I knew they were wide-awake in the dark, holding back their laughter, but I didn't say a word. I reached back to turn on the light, and the light switch was smeared with butch wax, the stuff we all put on our hair in those days. So I left the light off and went to bed in the dark.

I tried to stretch out in bed, and the boys had short-sheeted me. Somehow I was able to maintain my composure, straightening out the sheet and lying down again. Then my head clanked down on the pillowcase, which they had filled with Carl's weights. That was the last straw. They were snickering in the dark, and I was furious.

"All right," I yelled, "everybody up!"

I got them out of the cabin and had them running around the lake in the rain, and I could hear them laughing the whole way. My anger dissolved into defeat. It might have been the lowest moment of my camping career.

The next morning I went to ask Wayne Chastain, our camp director, for advice.

"Who's in control of your cabin?" he asked.

"I am," I said.

"Sounds to me like they are. They're trying to get a reaction out of you, and you're giving it to them. You need to get back in control. Do something positive. And when they do something just for a reaction, don't give them what they want. Stay in control, and do something completely unexpected."

I considered Wayne's advice all morning, and I decided that it might help me defuse the tension between Carl and Richard. I took each of them aside separately. "Richard," I said, "when Carl shoves you or trips you and you react in anger, he's in control of the situation. But when you maintain your composure, you're in control." I told Carl the same thing, to hold his temper when Richard made him the object of his jokes. For the next several days things between them settled down considerably.

Then on Sunday, it was Richard's turn to be the waiter for our table. When we ran out of gravy, he went to the kitchen for more. He was walking back to the table, and I saw Carl grin just a little. Something was up, but I didn't know what. Richard came back, and as he sat down Carl bumped his chair. Richard fell to the floor, and gravy went everywhere. Carl knew this would be the final straw, and in one motion he was out of his chair with his fists clenched, ready for Richard to come up fighting. I jumped up to step between them, and every eye in the mess hall was on our table. Richard was the only one in the room smiling.

He looked up at Carl and said, "You know, I've always liked gravy in my lap."

Now everybody was laughing except Carl. His fists relaxed and his shoulders slumped, defeated, and he walked out of the room. I followed him to a big tree, where we talked for a long time about the lessons we both had learned in my first few weeks as a camp counselor.

I never saw Carl again after that session. In fact, I never saw any of my first campers again. None of them ever came back to Ridgecrest—an indictment of my leadership. But even in defeat I learned lessons I could build on, and I believe those boys did too. I learned the truth of Romans 8:28, that in all things, no matter how bad they seem at the time, God works for the good of those who love Him, who have been called according to His purpose. He has spent forty-five years working good things out of my difficult beginnings.

CAMPER'S NOTE

Everyone needs a place of beginning, a place of growth, a place of learning and challenge. Whatever this place is, God uses it to mold each one of us into the man He wants us to be. Camp WinShape is that place for me. This place was my birth into the family of Christ. It is where I have grown in Christ and where I have grown physically. It also has built sound principles in my character and always produces a new challenge to go after. . . . If you haven't prayed all night long, you should try it. There is power in this kind of communion with God. Much of it is not even talking but listening to what He has to say. It was, to say the least, an amazing experience.

— Clayton Clark —

Tennis Lesson

Camp Ridgecrest hired me as a counselor in 1961 based on a recommendation from the youth director at our church, Robert E. Lee. I had been at camp for a couple of days before I had a chance to spend any significant time with the camp director, Wayne Chastain. By then I had already heard a lot about him. He had been in the navy, and he was a karate expert—a tough guy.

There were even some stories of counselors who had challenged him to fights, and he had taken care of them. Funny how stories like that get started and become part of the fabric of a camp.

Along about the third day Wayne took me aside for ten minutes or so and told me he had a lot of respect for me based on my recommendation, and he was counting on me to do my part with my cabin. I never forgot that little bit of encouragement. It's amazing how memorable an unexpected good word can be.

A couple of weeks later Wayne called me into his office. This time he wasn't smiling. I was the afternoon archery instructor, and the morning instructors had told him that I wasn't putting the equipment back in an orderly fashion. I hadn't been corrected too many times in my life except by my football coach, so Wayne's admonishment stuck with me. Unfortunately, I didn't let it affect other decisions.

Another counselor and I had been trying to find time to play tennis for over a week, and we decided to play that afternoon during rest period, when we were supposed to be in our cabins with our campers. We worked it out with our junior counselors, who were our assistants, to stay in the cabins while we played. I met my buddy and we worked our way through the woods down toward the courts as far from Wayne's office as possible.

Unfortunately for us, Wayne and four tribal leaders decided that day to go check on some of the cabins. "Johnson!" he yelled when he saw us from the path. "Where do you think you're going?"

I looked at my racquet, then at Wayne and smiled sheepishly. "Uh, lost and found?" I said.

"Get back to your cabin right now!"

I turned and double-timed it back to the cabin, where "rest time" had turned into near bedlam. All my guys, including my JC, were on the edge of their bunks watching one boy smear shoe polish on another. Both of the boys were both laughing, so I didn't have to break up a fight, but I did need to teach them a lesson. So I pulled them apart, then took the shoe polish and started putting it on the bigger guy to give him a taste of his own medicine.

Suddenly I heard Wayne's voice. "Johnson!" he yelled from the door.

I looked up, and there he stood with the tribal leaders. I was 0 for 3 in one day, and wondered how long it might be before they sent me home.

I'm amazed, looking back, at the patience Wayne and others had for me. I arrived at camp confident in my ability to lead boys, and I learned that I had a lot of growing up to do myself.

"I Will Never Leave You"

A long drive is a good time to think, and when Truett Cathy drove the family's brown station wagon out of the driveway in the summer of 1963, he had plenty to think about. For seventeen years he had operated his Dwarf House restaurant in Hapeville, Georgia. A second Dwarf House, which he had opened in nearby Forest Park, had burned to the ground in 1960, and its replacement, one of metro Atlanta's first true fast-food restaurants, did not allow the personal attention to customers that Truett had been accustomed to providing. Rather than disappoint patrons, he sold the second restaurant.

In the midst of his business challenges, Truett was diagnosed with colon cancer, requiring two surgeries to remove it. During the long weeks of recovery he thought often about his relationships and his responsibilities to his wife, Jeannette, and their three young children, Dan, Bubba, and Trudy. He fell on his knees before God many times during his ordeal, thanking Him for his life and the blessings he had received.

The experience led Truett to a deeper relationship with God and to a level of trust for his Creator than he had never known. "I learned the true value of life and was changed by that understanding," he later wrote of the experience. "Certain things happen in life that strengthen our faith and remind us of our need to put our lives in the hands of the Lord. I came out of the hospital a new creation, prepared to take on whatever life dealt, for I knew God would be with me."

He relied on that trust as he and Jeannette drove their children to camp for the first time in June 1963. Truett and Jeannette had learned about Camp Ridgecrest and Camp Crestridge through their church, First Baptist Church of Jonesboro. In its thirty-four years Ridgecrest had been the place of thousands of "mountaintop experiences" for boys, many of them away from home for the first time, experiencing God in the beauty of the high North Carolina mountains. Ridgecrest's sister camp, Crestridge, had been founded only eight years earlier, the same year Trudy was born, but it already had earned a reputation for providing a great camp experience.

The camps ran two five-week sessions, meaning that when Truett and Jeannette drove away, Trudy, who was seven-and-a-half years old, Bubba, who was nine, and Dan, who was ten, would not see their parents again until the middle of July.

They were more concerned for Trudy, who was small for her age and would be by herself at Crestridge. Dan and Bubba, even if they weren't in the same cabin, would see each other often and could encourage each other if either became homesick. Truett and Jeannette had hoped that the closeness of the two camps would allow the boys to see Trudy occasionally, but when they arrived, they realized that Interstate 40 separated Crestridge from Ridgecrest, and Trudy would most likely not see her brothers for the entire five weeks.

They didn't need to worry about little Trudy, who recalled later, "I think the only time I felt homesick was at night when I'd get in bed. We had to be quiet, and there was nothing else to think about, so I would think about home and Mom and Dad, and wonder what my brothers were doing over at the other camp.

"Sometimes it would be really cold up there in the mountains at night. We had screens in our cabins and I would hear the creek running nearby. I vividly remember listening to those sounds, and I'd curl up in my blanket and sometimes get homesick. I probably even cried a few times—cried myself to sleep. But I didn't dare let my counselor know I was homesick because I didn't want to run the risk that they might send me home. I wanted to stay really badly. So I would just suck it up and hang in there."

Trudy and the boys kept up with each other by writing letters back and forth between the camps, and she received lots of letters from home. And she loved everything about camp. On Sunday afternoon, two weeks into the session, campers were allowed to call home for the first time. Truett and Jeannette waited by the telephone for their three calls. Each time a counselor would place the call and then put the child on the line. They heard good reports from Dan and Bubba at Ridgecrest—about swimming and archery and crafts and about how much they missed home. Then Trudy called, and her first words were, "Can I stay for second session?" After just two weeks, she wanted to stay for the whole summer. Of course, Truett and Jeannette said no way, they wanted their little girl back home in three weeks not eight. Her call reminded them, however, that they had entrusted their children to God's care, and He could always be relied on to fulfill His promise.

Camp Challenges Reveal Character

Truett Cathy has an eye, an ear, and a heart for hurting children. Teaching Sunday school to thirteen-year-old boys, he has known many who have suffered from neglect at home because their parents were absent or too busy or distracted to offer the proper guidance. Truett gives these children more of his attention by understanding the importance of a positive adult role model in their lives.

After his own children had positive experiences at summer camp, Truett knew that these neglected children might benefit by attending Camp Ridgecrest and Camp Crestridge. He talked with their parents about the idea, and when some could not afford to send a child to camp, Truett offered to pay.

Decades later, the impact of Truett's decision is still felt by the children, their families, and the communities in which they live.

Jeff Manley was one such child. Years before Jeff stepped into Truett Cathy's Sunday school class, his parents had divorced, and then his father had taken his own life. Struggling through those difficult years, Jeff had extremely low self-esteem. He saw himself as a fat little kid with buckteeth who didn't do well in academics or athletics. Truett reached out to him in Sunday school and outside of church, as he does with so many troubled young people. Then he offered to send Jeff to Camp Ridgecrest for a session.

Jeff remembers the beginning of the transformation. The first two people he met, junior counselor J.J. McFerrin and counselor Carey Thompson, were men in his eyes. Carey was in college, J.J. was sixteen, and both had been long-time campers. They shook Jeff's hand, looked him in the eye, and spoke to him like a man. For the first time in years Jeff felt like he was where he belonged.

The following summer Truett sent Jeff to Ridgecrest again, and he began to bear fruit.

Today on the wall in Jeff's office there hangs a plaque for his year as president of the Chamber of Commerce. Other mementos commemorate his service as president of the Cattlemen's Association and the Georgia Breeders' Association. None of them is more important to him, however, than the certificate for "Camper of the Session."

"I was fourteen years old when I received it," Jeff recalls, "and when I did, Truett Cathy came up and congratulated me like I had won the Nobel Prize. I realized at that moment that maybe I wasn't a sorry excuse for a kid after all."

Jeff returned to Camp Ridgecrest the following summer and was "tapped out," or selected by his counselors, to undergo the test for achieving the highest rank, Little Chief. The rigorous ordeal required a ban of silence while he gathered wood, started a fire, and kept it burning through the night. At daybreak he would have to run to the top of Mount Kitazuma at a pace set by previous Little Chiefs running with the candidates, then he would write a 1,500-word essay on the impact of camp on his life.

Before beginning the test, Jeff and the other elite campers who had been selected, heard the Little Chief Charge, which we later adapted. It begins:

> In the process of growing up and developing into manhood, a boy is faced with many kinds and types of tests. Some of the tests he inevitably must face include tests of social adaptation, to check on his ability to live with and cooperate with others; test of physical endurance, to measure his natural growth and body development; tests of mental skills, to discover the amount of practical knowledge that he has learned throughout his daily life.

The challenges of summer camp revealed Jeff's character, and he passed the test to become a Little Chief. That experience shaped him and allowed him to shape hundreds of others in the years to come.

Gate of Opportunity

Truett Cathy believes in taking advantage of unexpected opportunities. "When I leave myself available to respond," he says, "I find that I am richly blessed."

In 1984, Truett took advantage of an unexpected opportunity, and since then he and thousands of children have been blessed by it through Camp WinShape.

The opportunity began with an invitation in the fall of 1983 to speak to business students at Berry College in Rome, Georgia. Truett noticed when he drove into campus that the sign at the entrance read: "Gate of Opportunity." Intrigued, he asked Dr. Gloria Shatto, president of the college, about the origin of the phrase. She told Truett about Berry's beginnings, how in the late nineteenth century Martha Berry had met some of the nearby mountain children, and after learning that they were not offered any schooling, had created the Berry School.

Dr. Shatto gave Truett a tour of the main college campus and then drove to the Mountain Campus, where Miss Berry had started her work and built her school through the early decades of the twentieth century. The beautiful old stone buildings looked to Truett like the ideal college setting—quiet and intimate, the stone evoking permanence. The Berry College president explained, however, that the old buildings would be locked up soon. For years they had been used by Berry Academy, the primary grades and high school that Martha Berry had organized before creating the college. Demand for the academy had fallen in recent years, and it was costing millions of dollars to keep the school open. The Berry trustees had decided to close it.

Truett was dismayed. He couldn't imagine this place, with its historical significance and obvious value, being mothballed. Dr. Shatto said the trustees hoped to find an alternative use for the Mountain Campus and were open to ideas.

Truett decided to take his wife, Jeannette, up to Berry to show her the campus. Perhaps the two of them might have a suggestion for its use. As they drove up they talked about Martha Berry and how God had worked through her to bring education and His word to hundreds of students over the decades. They stepped into Friendship Hall and Pilgrim Hall, beautiful old dormitories, then walked over to the Hill Dining Hall. Then they went over to Frost Chapel, where for nearly half a century students, faculty, and visitors had worshiped God. "I feel like I'm standing on holy ground," Jeannette said.

Truett and Jeannette knew that God had a plan for the Mountain Campus, and they believed they were a part of that plan. Truett met the next day with the Chick-fil-A executive committee and told them what he had experienced. The executive committee shared Truett's spirit of sharing but not his enthusiasm for the Berry Mountain Campus. They saw "a black hole" that would drain resources from other important and worthy opportunities. Truett insisted that they visit Berry. He also wanted his pastor, Dr. Charles Carter, to step onto the campus and experience what he and Jeannette had felt.

At the end of their day at Berry, Truett and Jeannette remained the only two convinced that God was calling them to this place. To everyone else the campus appeared to be a series of insurmountable problems. Even Dr. Carter tried to talk them out of it. Maintenance alone, Truett's advisors said, would be extremely expensive.

The Cathys agreed that the challenge was greater than anything they or Chick-fil-A could take on alone. But they knew God was in it, and with His active and direct involvement they would not fail. In the months that followed, God's plan would become clearer to them.

Truett's heart for young people aligned with Martha Berry's vision for molding the lives of youth. Truett believed God wanted him to maintain that purpose—to work with young people to shape winners, and from that vision came the name WinShape: shaping individuals to be winners. Through a partnership with WinShape and Berry College, more than 120 students would receive scholarships to the college and live at the Mountain Campus.

In December the Reverend Bob Skelton, who was on staff at Roswell Street Baptist Church in Marietta, spoke at a banquet at the Cathys home church, First Baptist of Jonesboro. Later he spoke at a youth evangelism conference in Macon where Bubba and Dan Cathy were playing trumpets in the Stone Brothers band. Bob had previously served as director of admissions for Shorter College in Rome and had also pastored a church in that city, and the Cathy brothers sought his advice regarding the WinShape College Program.

"I became excited as they told me their plans," Bob recalls. "I knew the campus and the city of Rome well. The following week they invited me to Chick-fil-A headquarters to discuss their opportunities, and over the course of several weeks in early 1984, I spent more time helping develop their vision for WinShape."

In June Truett asked Bob if he would consider directing the WinShape College Program. Bob and his family agreed to take the challenge, and they began the fall term with sixty-eight WinShape students.

In January Truett was visiting the Berry campus, and he asked Bob, "What are you planning to do this summer?"

"We'll be recruiting students, getting ready for fall, and taking a family vacation," Bob said.

"What about a summer camp?" Truett asked.

He made a convincing argument, telling Bob about the tremendous impact Camp Ridgecrest and Camp Crestridge had made on his children.

Bob didn't say it, but summer camp had been the furthest thing from his mind. How could they start a camp from scratch and have it up and running in five months? It was an impossible schedule, but Truett knew that "with God, all things are possible" (Matthew 19:27).

CAMPER'S NOTE

Camp WinShape is God's camp. He made this camp and He made it just for us. I hope Camp WinShape continues to touch kids' hearts and brings them closer to God.

— Dylan Fowler —

Meeting in Truett's Tree House

The long winding drive past the pond and through the woods to Chick-fil-A headquarters confirmed to me Truett Cathy's love of God's creation. The two-hour conversation that followed reminded me of his love for God's children.

Truett had invited me down to discuss the possibility of my becoming WinShape camp director. I wasn't looking to leave Ridgecrest, where I had been boys camp director for five years and general director of both Ridgecrest and the girls Camp Crestridge for another five years. But I couldn't pass up the opportunity to at least discuss the prospect of helping start a new camp. I was forty-three years old, more than twice the age of many of my camp staffers, and I had been working at the same camp since I was a teenager. If Truett offered the opportunity and I declined, I knew I would probably never leave Ridgecrest.

We met in Truett's fifth-floor office, which had a wall of floor-to-ceiling windows looking out into the forest. It was like sitting in a tree house. Truett's sons, Dan and Bubba, joined us, and we spent several minutes remembering their good times at Camp Ridgecrest years earlier. When we started the "interview" portion of our meeting, it was not at all what

I had anticipated. I expected questions about programs and goals, about my vision of a new camp. Instead we talked about life and family and relationships. I felt welcome, and they gave me the impression that they wanted me to be their camp director.

Truett was sixty-three years old when he interviewed me, twenty years my senior. If you had asked me that day, I would have told you that sixty-three was old—that my next twenty years needed to have the most impact of my life. Talking with Truett, however, I realized that there is no reason to stop, or even slow down, when we reach the world's definition of "retirement age."

Truett Cathy had big plans for WinShape—for college students, foster homes, and a children's camp. At the same time he would be expanding Chick-fil-A. Now, as I write this, I am sixty-five years old, and Truett is eighty-five. It's almost unbelievable to me to see the things he has accomplished in the past twenty-two years since that day in his office.

When Truett interviewed me, Chick-fil-A had about 300 restaurants. Today there are more than 1,300 Chick-fil-A restaurants.

When Truett was sixty-three, he had not yet built his first foster home. Today he has fourteen homes in which more than 140 children are growing up with two committed parents and calling him "Grandpa." When Truett was my age, the WinShape scholarship program at Berry College was in its infancy. Today more than 800 students have attended Berry on WinShape scholarships.

Truett has written four books and given countless speeches in the last twenty years. In fact, his speaking schedule is still busier than most young chief executive officers. Still, he hasn't stopped working, Truett never stops, and he inspires me to keep going full speed as well.

I did not fully capture Truett's vision for the WinShape programs as we sat together in his tree house, but I knew God was in his plans and I wanted to be a part of them. Then he described the WinShape Homes foster care program he envisioned and asked if my wife and I would be interested in helping. I squirmed in my chair as I formulated my answer. I believe foster parents have a special calling from God, and I had not experienced that call. But I didn't want to discourage Truett, so I didn't rule out the possibility of our becoming foster parents.

When I finished speaking, Truett, Dan, and Bubba were all called out briefly to deal with another issue. Sitting alone in Truett's office, I thought over what I had just said, and I knew I had to be totally honest. I had to tell Truett that we would not be interested in becoming foster parents, even if it meant losing the opportunity to become camp director. When they came back into the room, I told them, and Truett said that was absolutely fine. Their primary desire was to have me serve as camp director. I breathed a huge sigh of relief knowing that I had told the truth but wondering if another man might come in and better fit the Cathys' expectations.

I drove away that afternoon thankful for the time I had spent with Truett, Dan, and Bubba, and praying that God would open this opportunity for me. I had no idea that they were also praying—that I would be willing to leave Ridgecrest and help them start Camp WinShape. I thank God for answered prayers.

Building a Camp

They say Rome wasn't built in a day, but in a little over three months we built the WinShape camping program right outside of Rome. God had already laid the foundation. We had the beautiful Berry College campus and the financial support of Chick-fil-A. I brought my experience and a proven camp program. All we had to do was start and run our program like we had been running for twenty-two years at Ridgecrest.

I arrived at the WinShape Centre on March 1, 1985, and immediately began meeting Berry students and walking the land. From among the students would come the core of our summer staff; 80 percent of our counselors that first summer were Berry students. The land would provide opportunities for games and skills venues as well as inspiration for campers and staff by revealing God's awesome power through His creation.

I sought out and found Jeff Manley right away and sat down to have lunch with him. Jeff had become a Little Chief at Ridgecrest seven years earlier, and now he was a twenty-one-year-old Berry freshman. I was counting on him to become my right-hand man, and he didn't let me down. Jeff's experience as a camper at Ridgecrest proved invaluable. He understood the traditions and principles we wanted to bring to WinShape, and he knew how to work out important details like the secrets for building the council ring fire. He knew the Little Chief program, so he and I began mapping out how we would select and test our Little Chief candidates. Jeff was a full-time college student with a part-time job, and from March 1 until the last day of the last session of camp, he was completely devoted to WinShape.

The first thing we had to do was find campers, and we believed the best place to look was among the children of Chick-fil-A employees. We also knew that families were already making summer plans and we had to act fast. So we scheduled a Chick-fil-A family outing to show them what WinShape would offer, and on a Sunday afternoon less than a month after my arrival, more than two hundred people came. By that time Jeff had built a council ring in front of the WinShape Centre (where we continue to hold our closing ceremony) and set up a borrowed teepee. Jeff and Woody Faulk, who worked in the Chick-fil-A marketing department and was another former Ridgecrest Little Chief, along with David Salyers, agreed to be tribal leaders for a day. With war paint and Indian headbands for everybody, we divided into Apache, Shawnee, and Sioux tribes around the council ring. We sang every camp song we could remember and made up a few more, and by the end of the day we had generated considerable excitement among Chick-fil-A families.

The next week I hit the road and spent most of the month of April visiting families and churches, recruiting campers and counselors by selling the benefits of Camp WinShape. Bubba Cathy connected me with a dozen Chick-fil-A Operators around the Southeast who invited me into their homes to tell them and their neighbors about Camp WinShape. My first stop was Pensacola, Florida, where Steve and Linda Grossman, Chick-fil-A Operators who didn't know me from Adam, opened their homes and invited a crowd to meet me. Their son came to camp, and the next summer their daughter came too. The same thing happened with Operators and their friends in Jacksonville (David Bledsoe and his wife) and Orlando, and our momentum built quickly.

No "road show" is complete without photographs, and we had plenty depicting the beauty of the Berry campus. Camp Ridgecrest shared photos of their programs so we could show prospective campers some of our planned activities. I came back in May with the promise of applications in the mail and started interviewing for staff positions.

In the meantime, I had ordered equipment: canoes, archery equipment, .22-gauge rifles, arts and crafts supplies. I had a part-time secretary holding down things in the office, and Jeff and others were preparing the sites. Woody Faulk and Terry Carter, another Ridgecrest Little Chief, drove up from Chick-fil-A headquarters to help Jeff build our "in-the-woods" council ring. They hiked up Lavender Mountain to a spectacular spot, where they cleared the site and trimmed back enough limbs to give us plenty of room. When the counselors arrived in June, we were just about ready. We spent all of staff week with the final set-up of camp and getting to know one another. Then on Saturday, the children came.

We learned so many little things that first year that have made every year since then better. For example, we didn't specify what time children should arrive, so some of them came in early in the morning, others late in the afternoon. We had a hard time starting any organized activities with all the coming and going. The good news for us was that most of the children had not attended summer camp before, so they didn't have a standard of comparison.

Before long, though, they were running and playing, learning skills and songs—all the things camp is about. Laughter, we all learned, makes up for a world of little mistakes.

CAMPER'S NOTE

What makes WinShape so unique? It's God. He is so present. He has His hand in WinShape after all of these years, and the tapestry of lives that are formed in that place is amazing. The minute that you are reunited with a fellow WinShapers, there is magic. It is like no time has passed. And even if you've never met the person before, you have a wonderful bond because WinShape will never change in that respect.

— Amanda Bolton —

When I first came to camp this year I was trying to do everything right so that I would get tapped out for Little Chief. After the devotions and the time I spent with my counselors, I realized that getting tapped out is nothing compared with strengthening my relationship with God.

— Ryan Loftin —

Small Acts of Encouragement

We sent Timothy, who is our brother and God's fellow worker in spreading
the gospel of Christ, to strengthen and encourage you in your faith.

1 Thessalonians 3:2

Gavin Adams was ten years old when his parents brought him to Camp WinShape the first summer that camp opened. He was so excited and nervous that the rainy trip from Atlanta to Berry College didn't seem half as long as the three-mile ride from the highway through the woods to the Mountain Campus.

Then he and his parents hurried to get out of the rain and into Hill Dining Hall, where the counselors and I were greeting campers. I shook hands with Gavin and his parents, then said, "Let's meet your counselor." I turned and gestured toward a mammoth of a young man, 350 pounds, at least.

"Gavin," I said, "this is Killer."

Gavin looked up at Killer, then back at his parents. I could tell he was ready to get back in the car.

"Come on, Gavin," Killer said. "Let's put your stuff away and go swimming."

Gavin looked back at his parents one more time, hoping they might yell, "Run for the car!" They just hugged him and said they loved him, so he carried his duffel bag to his room and walked back into the rain to the pool with Killer and several other campers. Only years later did Gavin learn that his mother cried all the way home.

For the next ten summers Gavin came to Camp WinShape either as a camper or a counselor. His parents knew at mid-session parents' day that first summer that WinShape and Killer were just right for their son. Gavin ran over and hugged them, then said, "Gotta go," and ran off to play with other campers. And when his parents registered him for camp the next year, he requested that Killer be his counselor.

Today Gavin Adams is middle school director at Southside Church in Atlanta, and he often falls back on the lessons he learned at Camp WinShape. Reflecting on those years, he says, "It wasn't the big deal things that people tried to do for me at camp that made the biggest impact on my life. It was the little things that they probably don't even remember."

For example, Gavin was walking alone back to Pilgrim Dorm late one afternoon when he heard somebody call his name.

"Hey, Gavin, we have pizza up here. Come get some!" It was David Holsendorf, a counselor for younger boys in camp. Gavin was thirteen years old by then, and David was a college student, one of the coolest guys in camp. "And he thought enough of me to invite me to eat pizza with him," Gavin says. "That made me feel really special."

Another time Gavin was on the basketball court when David Preston, who was basketball skills director, said, "You've got a nice shot, Gavin."

Nothing big. Just a few words of encouragement that made all the difference for a young teenage boy. Another counselor at the ropes course told him, "Wow, that's the fastest I've ever seen on the zip line."

Maybe it was, and maybe it wasn't, but the words were the kind of encouragement that bolstered Gavin as he grew.

As a counselor a few years later, Gavin tried to create opportunities for encouraging campers. "I wanted to prepare my devotionals to be so powerful that every kid would want to run to the lake to be baptized. But they don't remember my devotionals any more than I remember the ones I heard from my counselors. What they remember is the small things, the unplanned things."

Gavin also learned through his experience that even though he was most effective through little unplanned actions, everything he did fit into God's bigger plan. And that was the greatest encouragement to him. "God has an idea of what kinds of things He would like for us to be involved in at different seasons of life," Gavin says. "At age ten, I was in a training ground for the student ministry I am involved with now. The experience of camp gave me a passion for working with kids and seeing their lives changed for Christ. And so much of that begins with what we say to young people. Everything we say and do has a positive or a negative impact on their lives. I want to be sure everything I say has a positive impact."

Sock War

When I was program director at Ridgecrest and coaching basketball at Spartanburg Day School, the headmaster of the lower school had a summer camp. I asked him his favorite activity at camp.

"Sock War," he said."

"Sock War, what's that?" I asked.

He explained how they did it, and I knew we had to try it at Ridgecrest the next summer. During staff week up there, we went to Table Rock, North Carolina, and the parking area was a mile from the top. I introduced Sock War to the staff, not knowing if it would work. I sent all of the counselors to the top of the mountain, where the fire tower would be their fort. I gave them thirty minutes to get up there and protect it. I gave them and everybody else two socks each filled with sawdust, and if they hit an opponent, they won points. If you got hit, you dropped your socks and reported to the scorekeeper, then got back into the game.

We had two other teams made up of central staff, tribal leaders, and JC's coming up the mountain, and their goal was to capture the flag from the counselors. The staff loved it, and Sock War became a big part of camp.

That first summer, some of our counselors thought they were in "Braveheart" instead of at camp, when it came to Sock War. One guy was in ROTC at college and wanted to be a general in the army, and he was a little over the edge in planning. He gathered trash cans for shields so he could control the hill. Then he found sapling trees and pulled them back to use as catapults. He got his whole army to put their socks in the saplings, and when the others attacked, he waited until just right moment to release them.

Standing out front like Napoleon, he watched and waited. Finally, when he could see the whites of their eyes, he cried, "FIRE!"

His lieutenants released the catapults, and the socks all fluttered to the ground like dead ducks. The war was over in five minutes.

We've changed the rules through the years, but one of the greatest aspects of Sock War remains its ability to level the playing field for the campers. Some may be smaller, others faster, but everybody has a skill that can be used to succeed.

Jeff Golden, a longtime WinShape camper, remembers fondly one of his first Sock Wars. "I was an Apache, and I 'killed' one of the generals on the other side. I can still remember that, the look on this guy's face when a little seven-year-old sneaks up and pops him with a sock. It sounds silly now, but it was big at the time."

CAMPER'S NOTE

Your word is a lamp to my feet and a light for my path.
Psalm 119:105

This year's verse, Psalm 119:105, took on a whole new meaning when I had to look for firewood last night. I discovered just how important a light is when you are lost in the dark. This verse not only tells us that God is our light. It also means we must be a light to other people who are lost in darkness.

— David Adams —

Trust the Rope

Robby Ross desperately clung to the sheer face of Mount Yonah. Up ahead of him Jeff Manley, the Sioux tribal leader, had played out slack in the rope—too much slack, Robby thought. If he slipped, he would fall three or four feet before the rope cinched down, jarring him to the bone and slamming him against the rock. He glanced around and felt like the coyote in a Roadrunner cartoon with nothing under him but three thousand feet of air. Those specks down below were buzzards circling, and that little bump on the horizon was Stone Mountain, sixty-five miles away.

He looked up, and Jeff sensed he was frozen. "You know what to do," Jeff said. "Just find your next ledge and believe."

Robby wanted to cry out like the man with the sick child who cried to Jesus, "I believe. Help my unbelief!" But he kept his mouth shut. Even here, there were style points to be considered. Down below the other guys awaited their turns on the rock. They were watching and listening. Robby was a kidder. His strength was making people laugh, but not at his own expense.

The Sioux tribe leaves camp for hiking, whitewater rafting, rock climbing and other adventures. All kinds of older kids sign up to be Sioux: athletes and little guys, but mostly teenagers looking for adventure. Athletes come to camp having been the big men on campus back home. They're big and strong, and they're confident of their ability to do almost anything by their strength alone. Little guys, on the other hand, never dreamed of playing high school football. Often their self-esteem is low because they've been the brunt of jokes all their lives.

Then they all look at the face atop of Mount Yonah—three hundred feet, like a vertical football field, except it's solid rock. It's so challenging that U.S. Army Rangers from Camp Merrill train there. Some WinShape campers have been reduced to tears just at the prospect of climbing the rock. Others are ready to take on the mountain and conquer it by brute strength.

Jeff had spent three days training his campers for the climb. They had arrived in camp on Sunday, and at daybreak Monday they were on the road to the Appalachian Trail, where they hiked for three days. Every time they reached a bald mountaintop, Jeff had them stop to take in the view. Then he told them to rub their fingertips against the rock. "Feel it," he said. "Understand it. It's just you and the rock."

On Thursday morning they found themselves at the base of Mount Yonah, with its bald face staring off to the southwest. The hike was easy, but as they stood before the vertical face, the constant chatter turned to quiet reflection.

"All right," Jeff said when they had removed their backpacks. "We're going to work on some easy climbs here before we go up the face," and for most of the morning the boys got the feel of being connected by the rope to Jeff, a certified rock climbing instructor, and the mountain itself.

"Lean back against the rope," Jeff called to Robby as he started up the easiest rope.

"Trust the rope. It will hold you."

Robby fought, trying to master the mountain with his strength. "You can't beat it," Jeff said. "You have to work with it."

Robby came down and a smaller boy connected himself to the rope, and the athletes began to see what Jeff meant. Instead of relying on his upper body strength, the boy let the rope and harness do the hard work while he used his legs to pick his way up the rock.

"Great job!" Jeff had called out. "Good climb!"

Now Robby was back in the harness looking up at Jeff, literally and figuratively. After three days and nights in the mountains, the camper knew his leader was the kind of man he wanted to become. He talked easily about his relationship with Christ, but didn't pretend life with Christ would be easy. "He will allow us to have trials," Jeff had said, "but never beyond anything we can bear. He will always provide a way."

Robby couldn't let him down. He saw a tiny ledge and reached up for it, then pulled. His foot found support below, and he was going up. He was going to make it. All of the campers made it to the top that day, and for each of them the experience would go with them for many years.

Now the dean of students for a middle school and a varsity coach, Robby tries to instill in his students and players the same lessons. "We take our senior football players on a rafting trip down the Ocoee River and get them out of their comfort zones," he says. "They learn to trust their guide and trust each other. They learn they can't do it by their own strength alone. And when they apply those lessons to their own lives, they realize like I did that they can trust God never to leave them or forsake them."

The Value of Time Shared

"O LORD, . . . I am slow of speech and tongue"
Exodus 4:10

We've had a lot of children with speech impediments at Camp WinShape through the years, but few were as severe as Robert Carpenter's. Robert stuttered so badly that at times he could hardly speak his own name. The first day of school every fall was always the worst day of the year for Robert, because when students went around the room introducing themselves, he froze up. Fortunately, he had good friends, and someone would invariably speak up and say, "This is Robert Carpenter . . . ."

I believe Robert's stuttering made him more sensitive to the needs of our campers and counselors. You see, Robert wasn't a camper when he came to WinShape. He was our first Apache tribal leader.

I met Robert when I moved to camp in March 1985. He was a WinShape scholarship student at Berry and had worked for Chick-fil-A. When I learned what he had accomplished, I knew he was the guy to work with our younger campers and their counselors.

Robert had started working for a Chick-fil-A unit in his hometown, Virginia Beach, Virginia, where he was a natural behind the counter. His warm, friendly smile attracted customers, who weren't put off by his slow speech. He smiles remembering when the phone would ring someone would say, "Robert, I'll answer the phone, you sell chicken." Selling chicken was what Robert did best. He sold chicken so well, in fact, that when a new Chick-fil-A restaurant opened in Clarksville, West Virginia, he was sent there to help with the opening.

From there he became part of the company's national marketing blitz team, traveling to cities where new restaurants would be opening, shaking hundreds of hands and doing advance public relations work.

All the while Robert was attending a community college back home. When he heard about the WinShape scholarship program at Berry, he applied and was accepted as a sophomore. He was twenty-two years old. I met him the following March and, as I say, he seemed a natural for Apache tribal leader. I had no idea, however, the effect our confidence would have on him.

"I have an outgoing personality," Robert says, "but because of my speech, I didn't say a lot sometimes. Then Truett, Dan, and Bubba Cathy, Bob Skelton, and Rick Johnson all accepted me for who I was. They didn't care how I talked. And neither did the children when they came to camp. Outside of my family and a few close friends, I had never experienced that before. That gave me tremendous confidence at a time when I didn't have much confidence in myself."

A highlight of that summer for Robert, and for me, was the modeling he experienced from Truett Cathy. "Truett came up to camp a lot that first summer," Robert recalls, "and he spent a lot of time with campers. He took time with counselors, mentoring them and showing all of us how we could make a positive impact on campers. And he listened. Truett Cathy is a master at listening. It's a wonderful gift from God that makes people feel comfortable with him. Having that example showed me how to model those things for the campers."

Robert continued to work for Chick-fil-A after he graduated from Berry. He loved going to work every day and never wanted to leave. Then in the early 1990s, he experienced a call from God to preach. "I thought I was losing my mind," he says. "There was no way I could preach a sermon." So he ignored the call and continued doing what he loved. But he couldn't get the call out of his head and his heart. So he called Truett, who invited him to come to Atlanta for several days. There he experienced again the compassion he had known at camp years earlier.

Robert and Truett talked every night in the living room after dinner, and the next day they rode motorcycles together. Robert couldn't believe how much time Truett was spending with him when he had a company to run.

He continued to feel God calling him, and he fought it with everything he had. Then Truett said, 'Robert, if God is calling you, you have to find out what He wants you to do.'" "But Truett," Robert said, "I can't talk. How can I preach?"

"God is faithful," Truett said. "Trust him." Then he took Robert's hands and prayed with him.

Robert left Atlanta as frightened as ever, knowing he would be leaving Chick-fil-A to go into the ministry. Then he was on a business trip one night before he left the company, and sitting in a hotel room he turned in his Bible to the book of Exodus. Moses stood before the burning bush and reeled off a list of reasons why he was the wrong man to lead the Israelites out of Egypt. His final excuse was, "O Lord, I have never been eloquent, neither in the past nor since you have spoken to your servant. I am slow of speech and tongue" (Exodus 4:10).

In that moment Robert identified with Moses more than any other Bible character. Then he read God's response: "Who gave man his mouth? . . . Is it not I, the LORD ? Now go; I will help you speak and will teach you what to say" (Exodus 4:11-12).

Robert followed God's call, attending seminary and then accepting a call from his first church. He asked the congregation to be patient with him—his sermons might take twice as long as other preachers. But Robert's congregation responded to his compassionate, caring spirit—the same spirit that had been modeled for him at Camp WinShape.

Today, after participating in a unique speech therapy progam, Robert stands in the pulpit and speaks without a stutter. "God used that program to change my life," he says. "But none of it would have been possible if people hadn't believed in me all those years ago."

CAMPER'S NOTE

During the first week of camp, God started putting great opportunities in front of me. He started telling me that if I would take my eyes off myself and look at other people, camp would be a lot better for all of us. So when I started doing that, camp was more fun, and I got along with other people better. This is my best year because God showed me how to be encouraging and helpful to others, and that makes everybody's Camp WinShape experience a good one.

— Jay Cook —

Speedy

"I tell you the truth, unless you change and become like little children,
you will never enter the kingdom of heaven."

Matthew 18:13

While I was on the road recruiting camp counselors, Truett Cathy asked Chick-fil-A Operators to spread the word about Camp WinShape among the teenagers working in their stores. He got a call back from a Chick-fil-A field consultant in Laredo, Texas, who told him that a high school junior working in the store there, David Earl Trejo, was just the kind of kid we were looking for. (They called him David Earl because there were several other Davids working in the Laredo store.) His parents were Baptist missionaries living in Laredo and serving a church just across the Rio Grande in Mexico, and David Earl had worked with them teaching vacation Bible school and Sunday school to the younger children.

He had already made summer plans to visit his uncle in Columbus, Georgia, and work at a Chick-fil-A restaurant there, but when he read the Camp WinShape brochure, he thought it might be fun to be a junior counselor. He didn't follow up, however, because he assumed junior counselors had to pay to go to camp.

David had just arrived in Columbus when the Chick-fil-A Operator there told him, "Mr. Cathy called and said he wants to meet you."

"Who's Mr. Cathy?" David asked.

He learned who Truett Cathy was and was told to pack a change of clothes; he would be staying overnight with Truett and Jeannette Cathy at their home.

As soon as Truett and Jeannette met David, they knew the Laredo field consultant had been right. He was just the kind of guy we needed at camp. He had a quick, bright smile and a maturity that had come from working with his parents at that little church in Mexico. There he had been friends with children living in homes with no electricity or running water, and he had experienced the gratitude on their faces when he offered them a snack and a Coke. David had seen first-hand what it meant to have nothing, and at sixteen he understood the true meaning of "gracias."

Truett asked him if he would like to work at camp instead of the Chick-fil-A in Columbus, and David said he would, but he had only brought one change of clothes. So Truett took him to Wal-Mart to buy clothes and linens for the summer.

David spent the night with the Cathys, and the next day Truett drove him up to Camp WinShape.

"I want you to have a good time," Truett told him, "and I also want you to have an impact on kids' lives." He had no idea how many lives David would impact over the next two decades.

The first thing I noticed about David Earl Trejo was his size. At five-feet-four, he was a foot shorter than me. I winked and told Truett, "We need a counselor, not another camper." David went along with the joke—I'm sure he'd heard it a thousand times before—and I quickly came to like this young man. I hired him as a junior counselor with the Apache tribe, our youngest boys.

It seems like almost everybody at camp gets a nickname, and some of the counselors started calling David, who was of Spanish descent, "Speedy Gonzalez," after the cartoon character known as "the fastest mouse in all Mexico." Now, that may sound like a stereotype, and it probably was, but there is also a lot of truth in the characterization. Speedy Gonzalez was a hero among mice, using his speed to help others more than himself. And he was always smiling. Likewise, David seems always to be looking out for the needs of others above his own—and he is almost always smiling. It wasn't long before the guys dropped "Gonzalez" from David's nickname, and he became just "Speedy."

I know some parents think Speedy is a silly name for a grown man. When he was getting married, Speedy's future in-laws asked if he didn't want to be known as David. "Are you going to want people to call you Speedy when you're fifty years old?" they asked. But Speedy is more concerned about his impression on young campers than adults. He wants the kids to know he's at camp to have fun, and he expects them to have fun too.

"My passion has always been younger kids," Speedy says. "Maybe that's because of my size, but I know that's where God wants me to be, because if they have a great first year at camp, they'll be campers for life. When they experience love, fun, and the joy of it all they come back."

Speedy came back the next summer as a counselor, and when he graduated from high school, he enrolled at Berry College as a WinShape scholarship student. Every summer from then on he was part of the camp staff. During those years he remained like a kid to the campers, but he also enjoyed bonding with his fellow counselors.

"That's what makes the summer," he says. "After the kids go to sleep, you can step out onto the porch for prayer time with other counselors, staff devotions, and just shooting the breeze with friends. You have to have good times with people your own age talking about things you can relate to. If I was having a bad day, that's where I sought advice. If we wanted to relax, we might play cards. Those relationships were priceless."

CAMPER'S NOTE

We always have fun no matter what. We have fun in the rain, in shine, in the morning, in the afternoon, at night, etc. No matter the conditions or what we are doing, it is going to be fun at Camp WinShape. We do the things I love here. If Camp WinShape is so awesome, I wonder how awesome heaven is going to be.

— Ryan Mickey —

Enduring Eagle

Blessed is the man who perseveres under trial, because when he has stood the test,
he will receive the crown of life that God has promised to those who love him.

James 1:12

Jason Byars had a lot in common with Jeff Manley. They lived one street from each other in Jonesboro, both attended the First Baptist Church, and both had been in Truett Cathy's Sunday school class. And both of their fathers had taken their own lives when the boys were young.

Despite the parallels in their lives, several years difference in their ages separated Jason and Jeff. So when Jason arrived at WinShape as a camper in the summer of 1985, he was surprised to find Jeff was a tribal leader.

"What tribe are you in?" Jeff asked.

"Navajo," Jason answered.

"No way, man, you gotta be a Sioux."

So they came to me and asked if Jason could switch to the Sioux.

I had known Jason for a couple of years. He was one of three brothers left by the passing of their father, and Truett had sent him to Camp Ridgecrest on scholarship. In February 1985 Jason called me at home in North Carolina and told me he wouldn't be coming to Ridgecrest that summer. "I'm sorry," he said, "but Mr. Cathy is starting a new camp, and I want to support him by going there."

Not many teenagers would have been as thoughtful as he was, and I was pleased to be able to tell him, "That's great, Jason, because I've been asked to be their camp director."

Knowing both boys' histories, I knew Jeff would have a strong positive influence on Jason in the wilderness. When they came back to camp after hiking the Appalachian Trail and climbing the rock face of Mount Yonah, Jeff recommended that Jason be tapped out for Little Chief. He was the only boy tapped out that session, and when they woke him up at midnight he would be going through the ordeal alone. He thought, "They have faith in me. I'm not going to disappoint them."

The weather was good, and Jason succeeded in lighting his fire and keeping it burning through the night. In the morning Jeff encouraged him and reminded him not to speak or make a sound. "Bite your lip," he said. "Bite your lip."

They took off up Lavander Mountain with another tribal leader setting the pace, Jason following, and Jeff running a few passes behind. "Keep it up," Jeff said. "Keep it up." As Jeff ran he remembered running up Mount Kitazuma years earlier. He saw himself as "the fat kid that nobody thinks can make it." He was one of twenty-one campers tapped out for Little Chief, and he was twentieth to start running up the mountain. By the time he reached the summit, however, he had passed nineteen others to finish second.

Now Jason was slowing down, and he just wanted to make sure he finished the run. After being awake all night, he was visibly weary. "Don't give up," Jeff said. "Persevere. Endure."

He did endure and made it to the summit of Lavander Mountain, where I was waiting. He looked at the ground while I led him through a devotional so he wouldn't be tempted to respond. I had stood at the mountaintop with a lot of young men striving to become Little Chiefs, but at that moment with Jeff Manly and Jason Byars, I'm not sure I had ever been with two who had endured and overcome more to reach the top.

We took Jason back down the mountain, where he wrote his essay telling what Camp WinShape had meant to him, and at the end of the day he became WinShape's second Little Chief. We gave him the Indian name "Enduring Eagle."

Today, if you visit Jason's office at Starr's Mill High School, where he is assistant principal, you will see sculptures of eagles, a photo of an eagle, and a poster with an eagle and the words "Dare to Soar." Jason keeps them, not to celebrate his accomplishment, but to remind him never to give up.

The Light of the World

Gus Denzik only vaguely remembers the candle in the cave, but Craig Craddock and other Sioux campers who were on that trip still feel its impact. Gus was a Sioux counselor, and he had led the campers deep into the cave. When they reached the bottom, he asked, "What if there were no light?" Then he turned off his flashlight and told them to turn off theirs. For several minutes the boys waited for their eyes to adjust. They never did. The cave was total darkness. Some of the boys closed their eyes, and nothing changed. Black was black.

Then Gus reminded the campers, "There is a light," and he struck a match and lit a candle. That tiny flame reflected in the eyes of every boy and illuminated the entire cave.

"You are the light of the world," Gus told the boys, quoting Matthew 5:14-16. "A city on a hill cannot be hidden. Neither do people light a lamp and put it under a bowl. Instead they put it on its stand, and it gives light to everyone in the house. In the same way, let your light shine before men, that they may see your good deeds and praise your Father in heaven."

Then he added, "One person can make an impact in the world just like this one flame allows us to see inside the cave."

Like all of our counselors, Gus is a light, although he prefers talking about the people who changed his life instead of the impact he has had on others. The son of a factory worker, Gus became disillusioned with college his freshman year and contemplated following his father into the factory. Then during spring break a friend arranged an interview with Bob Skelton for a WinShape scholarship. While he was on campus I interviewed him for a counselor slot, and instead of going home to Kentucky the following summer, Gus came to WinShape.

"God used the programs at WinShape and Berry to create a vision for me and show that He had something bigger for me," Gus recalls.

God's immediate plan was to work through Gus to touch our campers. During our first summer we had a high percentage of campers from children's homes. Truett had not yet opened his first WinShape home, so they came from other places. Many of them had been in trouble, and some of the older boys were bigger than their counselors. And most of them had never been camping.

"When we took them backpacking and rock climbing, they were experiencing God's world in a totally new way," Gus says. "They were working together, sweating together, and relying on each other. Then at night we would gather around the campfire and talk. We had started the day with a devotional and a prayer, and now we were wrapping it up with worship and more prayer.

The campfire ministry began to have a powerful effect on the boys.

"I always prepared a lesson for our time around the campfire," Gus says, "but that's not what the boys asked about. And that's not where the most powerful things happened."

One boy asked Gus, "How do you go back after you have crossed the line into sin?"

The flickering light reflected a tear on the boy's cheek, and Gus knew one would soon be rolling down his cheek as well.

"Your choice to be pure starts from this day forward," Gus said. "God will never discard you; Christ died for you."

The boy came to camp believing he was worthless because of his sin, but Gus convinced him that God loves him and cares for him. Then Gus and all the boys added a stick to the campfire in a ceremony of both sharing and leaving behind the past life as the light shone in all their faces.

Through Grace, God's Plan Emerges

God has used Camp WinShape as a training ground for several counselors who have gone on to full-time camp ministry.

James Himstedt was ten years old when his Baptist missionary parents were called to Brazil. One of the first families they met there were John and Trudy White and their children, who devoted ten years to missionary work in Brazil. The Himstedts lived about five minutes down the road from the Whites, and James grew up helping out by collecting eggs from their chickens or watching their dog when they were away.

When Truett and Jeannette Cathy visited the Whites for Christmas 1989, Truett met James and told him all about Camp WinShape. James had his parents' servant spirit, and he knew he wanted to come to the United States and work at camp. A high school sophomore, he would be just old enough to be a junior counselor the following summer. His parents told him he could go, but he would have to pay for his own round-trip airfare. James learned that his wages for working at camp would be enough for his ticket, so the decision was made.

For seven summers, all through his college years at Baylor University, James returned to work as a counselor at Camp WinShape, where God revealed His purpose for James's life.

"I had wanted to be a doctor and travel internationally and heal people," James recalls. "I wanted to make a lot of money, and that would allow me to give a lot back to God."

James did not realize how self-centered his life plan was until the summer after his freshman year at Baylor, when everything came crashing down for him. Near the end of summer I learned that he had broken several camp rules during his off time. I confronted him, and he admitted what he had done.

I had a choice at that point. I could have fired James, or at the least kept him from returning to WinShape the following summer. But James was a good man, and WinShape was a good place for him to grow up and learn about God's grace. I told him he could return the next year if he agreed to tell his parents what he had done, write a letter of apology to the camp, then admit his indiscretions to the entire camp staff and ask for their forgiveness at staff week before first session the following summer.

Back at Baylor James searched his heart and sought the answers to important questions: "Who am I? What am I about? What is important to me?" In the summer of 1994 he returned to WinShape, stood before the staff, and told us what he had done the previous year and what God had done to change him. In the process of that change, he said he realized that his goal of becoming a physician had been "too much about me. In my mind the career and money were mine to share with God, not His. I know now that God made me for service—service His way."

James believed God was calling him to a career in ministry to children through camp. That same summer he became friends with Corie Adams, a Berry College student earning her degree in equestrian science and managing the horseback program for WinShape. Like James, Corie experienced God's call to ministry through camp. In time, they realized that God had brought them together; they fell in love and were married.

"Real world" financial concerns led Corie to find a part-time job as a veterinary technician, and James started selling office equipment. Then I received a call from a camp in Alabama looking for a couple to serve as its directors. I recommended James and Corie, and they were a perfect fit.

In 2005 the Himstedts opened their own camp, Strong Rock, in the northeast Georgia mountains, where I know they will experience many years of God's blessings.

As they began this new time in their lives, James reflected on what it meant to leave his family in Brazil that first summer and come to WinShape, and the impact he hopes Strong Rock will have on their campers: "Camp gave me a wonderful sense of independence, maturity, and responsibility. I know it was tough for my parents to send their first boy, but it was incredibly beneficial for me. That's what camping does for campers, particularly at a Christian camp, where campers develop confidence in Christ to stand with them no matter what they face in the future."

Janie Bird

God has brought the right person to us at the right time more times than I can count. That was never more true than in 1986, when we felt ready to start a girls' camp program at WinShape.

Jane Doss had been teaching physical education at Berry College for more fifteen years and was extremely popular with the students. Plus, she had worked in summer camps just about every year since she was a teenager, taking off only a few years when her children were born. By the late mid-1980s she had retired from camps herself, although her husband, Jim, was still working summers as a program director in Mentone, Alabama.

I knew Jane was just right for us; her connections at Berry could help recruiting staff and securing facilities for camp programs. I asked if she would consider directing our girls camp, and like I had done two years earlier, Jane jumped at the chance to start a camp program from scratch. In many ways, God had been preparing her all her life just for WinShape.

Jane grew up Texas, and when she was a teenager she saw a brochure for a three-year program for counselors-in-training at a nearby camp. Her father knew a member of the camp council and said, "Maybe next year you can do that."

"Oh, but I want to do it now!" Jane said.

Her father said okay, and she cashed in a savings bond so she could be a part of the C.I.T. program for the next three summers. Her fourth year at camp she worked as a counselor and knew camp life was her calling.

She attended college in South Carolina. While she was in college she worked for two summers as waterfront director at Camp DeSoto in northeastern Alabama. In subsequent years she worked in every capacity at camps, including co-owner of a camp with Jim and another couple. Then she retired from camping and thought that part of her career was over. But it was only just beginning.

The early years of Camp WinShape for Girls presented many challenges we never faced up at the Mountain Campus. The boys had a designated area that was, at least for the summer, all theirs. The girls camp, on the other hand, was housed on the main campus of Berry College. Because college needs took top priority, Jane and her staff sometimes paid the price. From one year to the next they might be moved from one dorm to another. Dining facilities changed as well. The staff had to adapt in order to give the girls the best experience possible.

What they lost in control they more than made up for in spirit. They started in the Ford buildings, the English Gothic buildings you see as soon as you drive onto campus. It wasn't easy transforming a stone dormitory into an Indian motif, but Jane did it with yards and yards of burlap. Every door was draped in burlap to give it a teepee look.

Jane's nickname is another example of the girls' spirit. She had recruited several of her students to work as counselors, and they wondered what to call her. "Jane" didn't seem appropriate, especially when they would be back in her classes in the fall. But "Mrs. Doss" wasn't going to work in camp. Then Jane, like all of the counselors, received her Indian name. She was "Janie Bird" all summer, and when camp ended, Janie Bird stuck.

Classes started in fall, and the WinShape counselors continued to call her Janie Bird. Then other students picked up on it. "It seemed appropriate," Jane says. "Some of my colleagues might have preferred being called 'Dr. Doss,' but I taught the kind of classes where informality was more acceptable than in history or science class. I never had any breakdown of discipline or respect because of it."

Five years after she started the girls' program, Janie Bird had been so successful she couldn't balance it and her full-time teaching. By that time she had twenty years with Berry, and she couldn't walk away from it. So she retired, again, from full-time camping, but she has never left WinShape. Every session she comes to the pavilion to call the dance we have with the boys and girls. The campers who have been here in previous years can't wait to see Janie Bird again leading them in the newest dances. "How many grandmothers would you see on stage dancing at this stage of life?" she asks.

"I loved my career at Berry College. It was a wonderful place to be. But camp, emotionally speaking, has been closer to my heart. I have maintained much stronger relationships with WinShape than with my colleagues at Berry. Even though my part in camp is small, I cherish it. I've been very blessed."

A Shared Passion

I lost count years ago of all the marriages that have grown out of Camp WinShape romances. For obvious reasons, we don't encourage romance—in fact, we discourage it—but when the Holy Spirit has touched the lives of godly young men and women at WinShape, wonderful things have happened.

On Saturday night, midway through each session, we bring the boys and girls camps together for a dance, led by our first girls' camp director, Jane Doss. "Janie Bird" teaches the kids lots of different line dances, very few of which require boys and girls to actually touch one another. After all, our younger campers don't want anything to do with the opposite sex!

On one of those Saturday nights, God lit a spark out on the dance floor. Chantel was a pretty fifteen-year-old girl from Fayetteville, Georgia, who was dressed in white and dancing in the crowd. Gavin, who was also fifteen, was smitten, and tried all night to get close enough to ask her name. He finally did, but the music and laughter were so loud, he couldn't hear her well. He did hear her say she was from Fayetteville, Georgia, however, and that excited him, because his family lived in nearby Riverdale and attended church in Fayetteville. He went home from camp a week later determined to learn more about this special girl.

The first Sunday morning back home, Gavin asked the boys in his Sunday school class if they knew Shannel. "You mean Chantel?" they asked.

"Yes!" Gavin cried, "that's her."

"She's great," they said. "You ought to get to know her."

"I know," Gavin said, but he didn't know how.

Soon after that, Gavin's parents said they were moving to Fayetteville, and Gavin was left with mixed emotions. He hated leaving his friends behind, but he knew a few people at Fayetteville County High School, and he wondered if he might actually go to the same school with the beautiful Chantel.

The first day of school he walked into homeroom, and there she was. He stood in the doorway just looking, wondering how he could be so lucky and hoping she would remember him. Other students started filling in around Chantel, so Gavin made a beeline to the desk behind her. "Hi," he said. "Remember me?"

"From camp," she said, and his heart soared.

But before they could strike up a decent conversation, the teacher, Mrs. Yarbrough, said, "All right now, I'm going to arrange you alphabetically."

Gavin slid down in his desk. That ends that conversation, he thought.

"Chantel Adams?" Mrs. Yarbrough said.

"What?" Gavin asked as Chantel moved to the first seat. "You're kidding. Your name is Adams too?"

"Gavin Adams?" the teacher said, and Gavin floated to the seat behind Chantel.

Several months passed before Gavin invited Chantel out on a date, and their friendship grew on the foundation of a shared passion for the Lord and Camp WinShape. The following summer at camp, Gavin feared WinShape might become an impediment to their relationship. Chantel came to the Saturday night dance wearing the feather of an Indian Maiden, the highest honor our girl campers could achieve. Gavin believed he had worked hard enough to be tapped out for the Little Chief test the following week, but suddenly his pride was on the line. He would be embarrassed if he, too, did not earn the highest rank.

Few campers have been as determined as Gavin, and he did pass the test and become a Little Chief. But through the process, he realized that he had begun the test in the wrong frame of mind. Becoming a Little Chief or an Indian Maiden was not about "me."

"The physical tests showed me that it was about God," he says. "Through it I began to see how God was orchestrating so much of my camp experience."

Chantel and Gavin returned to camp the following summer and then both were on staff through their college years. The summer after they graduated they became the first WinShape couple to marry, and now God is moving them toward full-time ministry.

When I see Chantel and Gavin, Speedy and Julie Trejo, Tammy and David Preston, and the other married couples who met at camp, I think back to those Saturday night dances. Almost all of the children and teenagers out there in the crowd are having a good time that will become another memory from the WinShape experience. For a few of them, however, God orchestrates a beautiful life together built on a foundation of their love for Him and for WinShape.

A Tribe of Their Own

A little boy off at camp for the first time misses his momma. In fact, after a week of seeing almost no females at all, some of the boys at Camp WinShape even start missing their sisters. The smiling faces of the few young women on staff have brightened many days over the years.

We're blessed with a kitchen staff particularly sensitive to the boys, learning their names, joking with them, and planning meals they will enjoy. Karla Phillips and her crew in the early years of camp helped set that standard. For a couple of years we had relied on Berry College food services to prepare meals in their facilities and bring them up to Hill Dining Hall. Then Karla and her staff, all college students who had worked for Chick-fil-A and knew their way around a kitchen, asked if they could plan and prepare meals themselves. They had seen what the boys liked and didn't like, and they proved their mettle on the first night the boys arrived, serving chicken fingers, green beans, and mashed potatoes. That would be our first-night menu for the next seventeen years.

The girls went out of their way to make sure the serving line was a joyful experience. They made up their own songs and sometimes came around to give a boy a hug. "We were sweeter than their counselors," Karla recalls.

After a while, however, the girls realized that the campers had something they didn't have—a tribal identity. How could they ever earn the respect of these boys if they didn't have their own tribe? They needed their own songs and chants. They pondered their dilemma, then saw the answer up on the kitchen shelf. They would be the Mazola tribe—a little corny, but the boys loved it. And when the chants started echoing through the dining hall, the Mazolas could keep up with the best of them.

Like most of our camp staff, what Karla remembers most about camp are the relationships formed over the long, hot summers. "Some nights I asked myself, 'Why do I love this?'" she says. "We got up early every morning and went to bed exhausted late every night. There was no air conditioning in the dining hall or the dorm. We were physically depleted. And yet, every day I thought, I am part of something way bigger than I am—way bigger than anybody here. I'm part of something that is making a difference in lives. That's huge. When you see a little boy smile or give him a hug when he's homesick, it's a special experience. I hope they remember that experience; I hope somehow those experiences helped shape them."

Through those experiences Karla and the campers became part of the same tribe, a tribe of love, and they will always be a part of it.

CAMPER'S NOTE

Each day is a journey, and we learn to enjoy that here. Bad steps and good steps in the journey are still steps for God, and that is what our life is about. No matter how bad that day's journey is, it is still a good journey, for we have become closer to God during it. Camp WinShape taught me how to enjoy each step rather than bask in the misfortunes along the way.

— P.J. Ross —

Alathea : Truth

In her fourteen years at Camp WinShape, Carrie Theobald learned how to make dreams come true. "I learned that with God, nothing is impossible," she says. "Sometimes you can't do it by yourself, but if you find a way to include others, you can tackle a dream."

When Carrie came to WinShape as an eleven-year-old camper, she quickly learned that she would have to get along with girls whose backgrounds were different from hers. "That was the first year of girls camp, and there were a lot of girls from children's homes, a lot of scholarship campers like me, and a lot of campers whose parents had good incomes."

Carrie began to experience the team building and the strength she received through others, but she never dreamed that strength would someday help her perform for audiences all across the United States.

After several years at camp, Carrie joined the Cherokee tribe, which spent most of its time away from camp, hiking, rock climbing, and whitewater rafting. "We were already bonding when we were at camp, but with the Cherokees, trust became a much more important part of the experience," she recalls. "We learned to be dependent and independent at the same time, knowing when to be a leader and when to be a follower. The exercises we had done on the ropes course back at camp became real life out in the woods."

Then came the day she had to perform the Heimlich maneuver on a camper out in the woods. Miles from the nearest road, Carrie relied on her training to save a life. Even as she performed the procedure, Carrie understood that her life might just as easily be in the hands of any of the girls in the woods with her.

In that spirit of interdependence, Carrie went to college and in 1997, while leading a Young Life group, began singing with two friends. Christian singer/songwriter Rich Mullins heard them and introduced them to a producer, and they were on their way.

The girls called their band Alathea, which is the Greek word for truth. Carrie was still working at WinShape every summer and leading a Young Life group back at college. Then came the concerts. "I don't know if I would have had confidence to go on stage if I hadn't gone to Camp WinShape," Carrie says. "I learned how to work hard and make dreams happen, to see a vision and carry it through."

She remembers particularly a concert for a youth group in Indiana, describing Alathea as "hillbilly girls from Tennessee." The audience, on the other hand, might be aptly described as "grunge," with lots of leather and more than a few dog collars and fishnet tights.

Carrie later told journalist Joe Montague, "There didn't seem to be a lot that we could connect with, but the amazing thing is once we started playing, the girls that we were terrified of sat down and engaged and listened. We had this great hour of time with these girls with whom it first appeared that we shared nothing in common. Afterwards the youth minister told us the year before they had a punk band and the kids were in and out the whole time. He said this was the first time that the kids actually sat down and were engaged the entire time. It was pretty humbling. Regardless of our backgrounds we all have this connection that makes it work."

The Great Chippewa Massacre

We've had several versions of outdoor camping at Camp WinShape through the years: under the stars, large tents on platforms, smaller tents on the ground. And in the 1990s, the girls camped in Conestoga wagons. Jeannette Cathy had visited Hume Lake Christian Camps in California, where they used big wagons like the ones that had brought settlers across the country. They were big enough for several bunk beds—just right for a tribe to sleep outside and have some protection from the bugs and rain.

Bob Skelton contacted Hume Lake to learn about the wagons, and the camp director offered to give us ten surplus wagons. But shipping costs would be so high, Bob thought it would be better for us to build our own.

We did, and the first one looked like Noah's Ark. Plus, we didn't have wheels. The carpenters made adjustments to the design while Bob searched for wheels. He visited an Amish wheelwright in Tennessee, who repaired wheels but did not build them and would not reveal his sources. Then Bob called Dollywood theme park, where he remembered having seen a stagecoach years earlier. From there he was directed to another wheel repair shop that did not manufacture wheels. Finally he found place in Ohio where they made wagon wheels. It was within twenty miles of a Chick-fil-A restaurant that was under construction—important because the truck delivering kitchen equipment could bring back wheels and axels. Bob placed an order for wheels and axels for four covered wagons, and we had our first Conestogas. Soon we had a dozen, and the girls' tribes took turns sleeping in them.

It was only a matter of time before the circled wagons became an obvious target for a tribe of Indians, and Lori Crawford was just the counselor to lead the charge. Lori was with the Cherokees, our oldest campers, and one night when her tribal leader and fellow Cherokee counselors had the night off, she put her plans into action. She called her tribe to a makeshift council ring and announced, "All right, go get your camouflage and your face paint, get your water guns and water balloons, get whatever you've got because tonight we're going to raid those wagons!"

The Cherokees ran back to their cabins and loaded up, then gathered back outside.

"Are you ready?" Lori called.

"Ready!" the girls yelled.

"All right, then, the only way we're going to succeed tonight is with Mission Possible." So the girls mixed eighteenth-century war paint and twentieth-century television as they tiptoed across the Berry campus singing the "Mission Impossible" theme song until they saw the wagons off in the darkness.

"Shhh!" Lori said, and all the girls gathered around their leader.

She whispered to the Cherokees, "Surround the wagons, and on the count of three, jump out guns blazing and squirt to kill the Chippewa. Massacre those Chippewa."

Meanwhile, the young Chippewa were in their wagons going about their business, getting ready for bed. Their tribal leader, Julie Trejo, was standing in the center of the ring of wagons talking with "Janie Bird" Doss, director of the girls' camp. Unbeknownst to the Cherokees, Lori was leading them into an ambush.

"One, two, three!" she whispered, and the teenage campers with their Indian war cries raced toward the wagons with guns squirting and water balloons flying. The first face Lori saw was Janie Bird, and her life flashed before her eyes. In that instant, she knew her camping career was over. But without regard to herself, she thought to save her warriors. "The Bird!" she cried. "It's the Bird. Retreat!"

Instantly, the Cherokee tribe turned and retreated to their cabin, washed off their face paint as fast as they could, shut off the lights, and dove under the covers. Lori never slept that night. Instead, she waited and waited for the door to open and Jane to step in and fire her. Dawn came and Lori thought, "I didn't get fired. She must be waiting for the tribal leader meeting this morning. But after breakfast Lori walked into the meeting and Janie Bird smiled and asked, "Have a good night?"

"Uh . . . uh," Lori stammered and never gave an answer. Janie Bird just smiled. She always seemed to know when to circle the wagons (seldom), when to come out guns blazing (almost never), and when a simple knowing smile could remind our staff leaders that they carry a heavy burden of responsibility. But there is also room for fun at Camp WinShape.

The Language of Forgiveness

Before he came to camp, Taylor had already slept under the stars more nights than he could count. And for many nights he had slept in a room alongside a bunch of other kids, so having lots of other children around was nothing new to him.

Still, he was nervous when his parents brought him to WinShape for the first time. He had never been to a real camp.

Taylor, you see, had grown up in Russia, with a destitute mother and siblings, and for four years they lived under bridges, in barns, and outside gas stations—wherever they could find shelter. They traveled from village to village, and Taylor would work for a farmer or a family to earn a little money or some food for the family. He was nine years old when he decided he'd had enough of the beggar's life, and he asked a family where he was working if they would take care of him. He wanted to stay in one place and maybe even go to school. The family agreed, and also said they would take his sister, but she decided to stay with their mother. That was the last time Taylor saw his Russian family.

For three years Taylor lived with his adoptive parents, until their son tried to stab him with a pitchfork. The next day Taylor moved to an orphanage.

That orphanage was the place where Mark and Le Ann Dakake came to adopt a Russian boy, and for several days, while they going through the process, they watched Taylor interacting with the younger children. Le Ann was struck by the boy's sensitivity, and when the Dakakes returned to the States, she began writing letters to Taylor. She hoped they could eventually adopt Taylor, but she didn't mention that possibility in her letters for fear they would raise false hopes. What Taylor remembers most about their correspondence was that Le Ann introduced him to the love of Christ. "I didn't believe in Christianity," he recalls. "I thought God hated me. I was an orphan, and I had nothing to look forward. That was just my life."

In 2000 the Dakakes came to take Taylor home. They adopted him into their family in Acworth, Georgia, and a few months after his arrival in the United States, he was a WinShape camper.

Taylor's English was minimal, but he says that was not a problem. "The counselors were really welcoming and Christlike, and somehow they were able to understand my English. They included me in every activity and put me in situations where I was forced to interact with other kids. That helped me improve my English and gave me leadership skills. From the first day I started liking it, and by the third day I was relaxed."

Taylor says his counselors also picked up on the themes of Le Ann Dakake's letters to him. "I was a Christian then, but not fully following Christ. When I came and got surrounded by Christian mentors, they taught me the Christian aspects of leadership and learning. If we played an activity, they tried to relate that to a Christian perspective. We played flag football, and they talked about teamwork and being united with Christ as a team. That made it easier for me to understand when they spoke it in the simplest language."

Six years after arriving in the United States, Taylor enrolled in Berry College as a WinShape scholar. By then he had worked as a counselor at camp for two years, and he tried to instill in his campers the importance of the little things in building character.

"I want them to learn by example," he says. "Like when I walk to the dining hall or WinShape Centre, I stop and pick up any trash I see along the way. Sometimes I will set up a contest and let the campers earn points by picking up the most trash. That way they see me doing something, and I try to motivate them to do it too."

Through the years Taylor has also tried to let others see an example of forgiveness. "When I came to America, I was struggling with forgiveness. I hated my mom in Russia for what she put me through. Then I listened to a speaker who talked about forgiveness like Christ's forgiveness, and as I thought about that I realized that if it weren't for my mom in Russia, I wouldn't be in America. I would have no life, no future. I had to forgive her. God brought me through all of that to where I am now. He had a bigger plan that I didn't see, and now it is a blessing to find out how God is working a miracle in my life."

CAMPER'S NOTE

In the Sioux tribe at Camp WinShape we were loaded with more responsibilities. We had to cook our own food and set up our own shelters. We also had responsibilities related to devotions. We had to find good verses and dig deep to explain them to the rest of the tribe. We learned a lot more, and I began to understand the depth of God's purpose. I finally accepted that whatever God has planned for me is best, whether it be meeting my goals or not. I learned to fully rely on God no matter what was happening.

— Grant Stauffer —

CAMPER'S NOTE

During devotion time, when the counselor is reading a Bible verse, I love to mark them in my Bible and write a note about what was talked about. During the school year, when I get home from school, I like to read those Bible verses and, especially if I had a bad day, I renew my strength.

— Daniel Graddy —

On the Mountaintop

Peter said to Jesus, "Lord, it is good for us to be here. If you wish,
I will put up three shelters—one for you, one for Moses and one for Elijah."

Matthew 17:4

It took a while for Seth Houser to make it up to the mountaintop, but once he did, he never wanted to come down.

Seth joined the WinShape staff in midsummer 1998 after graduating from high school. He missed staff week, and although he made friends quickly, he never felt in sync with the flow of camp.

"It takes time for a counselor to understand who he is," Seth says. "Your first instinct is to be buddy-buddy with all the campers—to be Mr. Cool Counselor. But then you have to discipline a camper, and he says, 'But I thought you were Mr. Cool Counselor!'"

Seth came back the next summer, and he enjoyed working with the kids and the challenge of providing spiritual leadership. "I was like most young Christians," he recalls. "I was saved when I was seven, and I knew a lot about Jesus. But I didn't really know Jesus."

During Seth's third summer at WinShape, everything changed. It started early in the summer when a camper ran over to him and said, "Hey, Seth, I'm still having my quiet time every day!"

Wow, Seth thought, God really is using summer camp to work on these boys.

"My attitude changed at that moment," he recalls. "Until then I thought my job was to help the kids have a good time, give them a good positive experience, and teach them good character-building through Bible study. Suddenly I realized that I had been missing that boat—I understood the power of camp to reach people for God's kingdom."

From that day forward Seth saw camp as a mission, not a job.

A few weeks later, Seth's tribal leader had to have surgery for a hernia, and we asked Seth to take his place. Seth took advantage of that unexpected opportunity to grow into greater responsibility.

"Little kids live their parents' religion," Seth says. "They go to church when their parents go, and follow their parents' lead. Summer camp gives them a chance to get away from their parents and spend time alone. They can make their own choices. Counselors, who aren't much older than they are, have a tremendous impact on them. They look up to their counselors and listen to them.

"At camp they are alone on a mountaintop with God with daily quiet time, night time devotionals, and sometimes intense Bible study."

Over time Seth began to see God changing the lives of his campers, and he was thrilled by the experience, so much so that he began to consider camp leadership as a career. Then during his senior year in college, Camp Arrowwood in the Smoky Mountains brought him on as camp director.

"Our program is smaller than WinShape, forty-eight kids with weekly sessions, but the opportunities and responsibilities are the same," Seth says. "For these children, some of their strongest spiritual moments occur at summer camp. They're following us up the mountain, and that's an awesome responsibility—one that I want for the rest of my life."

From Wilderness to Wilderness

Tammy Lyttle grew up in the South American jungle. The daughter of missionaries to Suriname, she lived in a thatch-roof hut on stilts about two hundred miles from the nearest large city. The ultimate childhood in the ultimate wilderness, she says, was swimming in the river and exploring the jungle with her friends. Every fourth year the Lyttle family came to the States on furlough, and though Tammy and her younger brother and sister enjoyed visiting the North, they couldn't wait to get back home.

Tammy's junior year in high school fell on a furlough year, and when it was time to return to Suriname, her parents thought it would be best for her to stay behind and finish school in the States. So Tammy enrolled in a boarding school in North Carolina and began working at a nearby Chick-fil-A. The store Operator told her about the WinShape College Program at Berry, and when Tammy applied, she was accepted as a WinShape scholar.

You might expect the daughter of missionaries to have a strong servant spirit engrained in her. Tammy says that was not the case with her. Her parents were passionate about their ministry to the indigenous people of South America. Tammy, however, says she did not share that passion as a child. She loved her friends and her life there, but she did not "take ownership" of her parents' mission work.

Then she came to work at Camp WinShape. Several WinShape college students had planned to work at camp, and Tammy decided to join them. When I hired her to work at the girls' camp, her plan was to "hang out with my friends and have a good time with the kids."

"I had no clue what camp would do in my life to transform me personally," she says. "For the first time in my life I was put in a totally serving posture, I was focused on and responsible to the needs of others, and I found it to be very natural for me."

I don't remember if we deliberately placed Tammy with Chippewa One, the youngest girls in camp, or if God quietly nudged us in that direction, but the wisdom of that decision soon became clear. Whenever the older girls or other counselors talked about American pop culture, Tammy was lost. She had completely missed Pac Man, Donkey Kong, and Rubiks Cubes, Dallas, Dynasty, and Star Wars. It became a running joke—"It's a Suriname thing," she would say when she missed a punch line.

But with the little girls in her cabin it didn't matter. Most of them were away from home for the first time in their lives, and spending hour upon hour outside with no television was a total wilderness experience for them.

If the little girls were undergoing changes in their newfound "wilderness," Tammy was experiencing a radical redirection toward her natural inclination to serve.

So natural was that servant spirit and desire to serve others, in 1991 she helped create WinShape Wilderness, where she says "change, or spiritual transformation, is what we strive for in every program we facilitate."

This is Tammy's mission work. She is not in the jungle like her parents, but she works in the wilderness swinging from ropes, climbing rocks, and canoeing down rivers, creating opportunities for God to transform the lives of others the way He transformed her during her first summer at camp.

A Call to Serve

Angela White, Trudy and John's daughter, was a sophomore in high school when she and her parents started discussing the possibility of an overseas trip for her, perhaps to China, following her graduation. For the next two years they made plans, and as graduation approached, details for a trip China fell into place.

Then the SARS virus broke out in Asia, cutting off most travel to China, including Angela's trip. Angela and her parents considered other travel possibilities, then the conversation turned to camp. Angela told some of her memories as a camper at WinShape, and Trudy recalled her days at Crestridge. In the midst of their reminiscing, they decided to spend a week together at each camp, volunteering to do whatever the staff needed. The leadership at both camps welcomed the idea, so when summer came, Trudy and Angela drove up to Camp Crestridge.

Trudy's memories flooded back and spilled over as they drove up the mountain. "My first summer at camp when I was seven," she said, "I always wanted to be the first one in the lake for swimming. The water runs off the mountain into the lake, and it's always icy cold, but I didn't care. And sometimes when I jumped in, there might be a little water snake in there with us, but we would just push him aside and keep on swimming."

Trudy wonders how she and Angela ever got any sleep the first night of their visit because the stories went on and on. Trudy sang every silly camp song she could remember, and when she finally ran out of stories and songs, things got quiet. Then there was the familiar sound of the creek spilling over rocks. That sound took Trudy back to her nights as a seven year old, so far from her mother and father, and so close to God. And with her daughter in the next bed, she slept.

Morning came, and Trudy and Angela spent the week running errands, cleaning the dining hall, anything the staff needed, and then, suddenly, the week was over and they were in the car driving to WinShape.

Trudy began to realize how little she knew about WinShape. The Whites had been living in Brazil as the camp started and grew. Almost everything she knew about the camp she had learned through Angela's experience. As they approached camp, Angela's stories came faster, along with her own silly songs, as she relived her own special camp days.

When they arrived, they took on duties similar to those they had at Crestridge— whatever the staff needed. Then Amanda Lepper, girls camp director at WinShape, asked Trudy to speak to the girls when they gathered around the campfire. Trudy agreed, and when she looked at those 200 or so girls and then to the mountains beyond them, she was suddenly touched by the feeling that God was moving in that place. As she spoke, she tried to listen, and by the time she sat down, she knew that God had her there for a reason. He wanted her more involved in Camp WinShape. At the end of the week Trudy and

Angela drove back home to Virginia, and Trudy considered the possibilities.

Over the next several months, John was experiencing a call from God as well. After almost twenty years of service through the International Missions Board of the Southern Baptist Convention, where he was at that time executive vice president, John was being called away. Unlike their call to international missions two decades earlier, this time the Whites didn't know where God was leading them.

"I'm waiting to see what happens next," John told the mission board. "What I do know is that God doesn't always work at our frantic pace. He works on His time schedule. We have no plan B, only plan A—and that's to do what He asks us to do."

They moved home to Atlanta to wait, and Trudy followed up on her experience at camp by calling Amanda Lepper to offer her support. "I want you to know I'm here for you," she said, "and I want to be your prayer partner and support what you're doing at camp."

Amanda, who was struggling with her own call, said Trudy's words were a great encouragement to her. A few weeks later she called and said she had decided to leave WinShape to pursue a master's degree and go into teaching full time.

"Oh, Amanda," Trudy said, "you can't leave camp. I'm sure one of the reasons God brought us back to Atlanta was for me to be an encourager for you."

Amanda did leave, and through the days Trudy realized what God might have in mind for her. Her family began telling her that she might be the one to step in for Amanda, at least until they could another director for the girls camp.

The possibility frightened Trudy. She had never worked at a camp beyond the junior counselor level. But she also knew that God had taken her through other experiences, particularly in Brazil, where she had no idea what to do, and yet she had remained dependent on Him. So she prayed. And prayed. And at the end of her prayers, she knew God wanted her at Camp WinShape for Girls—not for a season or two until they found a permanent replacement, but for the long term.

She told me and other camp staff, "If you'll help me learn the ropes here, I'm certainly willing."

CAMPER'S NOTE

I have the hardest time explaining WinShape to friends because it is so unbelievable. You have to experience it yourself to understand the amazing worship times, the small-group time in the cabin with your counselor, and the relationships you build. The atmosphere is like a different world and you focus on your relationship with God, and you go away having made the closest friends you can imagine.

— Beth Turner —

Passionate Starlight's
First Indian Dance

Trudy Cathy White knew she was the new kid on the block in so many ways. She and her family had been living in Brazil as the WinShape Camps grew in their early years, and unlike her brothers, Dan and Bubba, she had not participated first hand in the development. She never aspired to be a camp director; the Lord had simply laid it in her lap. So she was a little relieved when her first session started smoothly, for the most part, with only a few minor glitches. By Sunday she was looking forward to her first council ring on Wednesday night.

She called her tribal leaders together for a planning session, and they explained the format. The girls would wear face paint and feathers in their hair indicating their tribes. A silence ban would be imposed, and they would walk single file to the council ring area. There, the tribal leaders explained, Trudy would perform an Indian dance.

"I'm sorry, what did you say?" Trudy asked.

"At the council ring," explained Kindhearted Chameleon, "the camp director performs an Indian dance for the camp."

Trudy could feel her stomach rising up toward her throat. "By myself?" she asked.

"Absolutely. You're the leader."

At that moment Trudy knew she had made a big mistake. She didn't know anything about Indian dances. She had never even seen an Indian dance.

"Do I have to do this?" she asked.

"It's a camp tradition," she was assured. "The camp director always does the Indian dance for the whole camp."

Trudy was formulating the words in her mind: "You know what? I think I'm going to break that tradition." But she couldn't bring herself to say them. Deep inside she knew how important it was to blend in with the girls and not feel like there was a generation gap because she was a mother and soon to be a grandmother.

"You know," she said standing up and feeling her spirits rise, "I'll do it."

"Good, good," the tribal leaders said, and Trudy could feel her chest tighten, making it harder to breath.

Trudy awoke the next morning, still two days before council ring, feeling sick. Her son John was at camp that day so she asked him, "You've been to council ring at boys camp; can you help me come up with what an Indian dance might look like?"

They got behind closed doors and John showed Trudy a few Indian dance steps. Trudy tried them out, but she knew it wouldn't work. She just hoped none of the girls laughed out loud.

With Wednesday came the rain—so much rain that council ring had to be moved to the gym. Trudy's first council ring and Indian dance wouldn't even have a fire. She stood off to the side reflecting on the line of camp directors who had gone before her. Jane and Julie and Amanda had all stood where she was standing and made it through. She would make it too. Then Kindhearted Chameleon stepped out in front of the girls and introduced her. "Now Passionate Starlight will perform her first ever Indian dance for the camp." And the girls, true to their silence ban, watched mute as Trudy began her dance.

Trudy did her best to follow John's instructions, and wondered as she finished if any of her predecessors had spent less time than she just had with their Indian dances.

And when Trudy learned that it was all a ruse, that she had been the first camp director ever to do an Indian dance for the entire camp at council ring, the only emotion that exceeded her short-lived anger at the girls for setting her up was her relief that she would never have to do another Indian dance.

New-Found Leadership

Jenny Gabrielson laughs when she looks at the letters from camp that her parents saved, but she wasn't laughing at the time. Jenny was ten years old the first year she came to Camp WinShape, and she was terribly homesick. She wrote home almost every day telling her parents that she cried herself to sleep at night. She begged her parents to come and get her. She cried as she wrote those letters, and when a teardrop hit the paper, she circled it and labeled it: TEAR.

In those days parents visited camp on Sunday, midway through the two-week session. Jenny decided she would go home with her parents and skip the second week of her session. "What are you doing?" her counselor asked when she came into the cabin and saw Jenny putting clothes into her suitcase.

"Just organizing my things," she said. But she was packing to leave.

When the Gabrielsons arrived, Jenny met them at the door and said, "I'm ready to go."

The easy thing to do might have been to scoop up their little girl and race for the highway, but her parents said instead, "Not yet. Show us around camp first."

So Jenny showed them where she was learning new skills, she took them to the stables, and she showed them the pool. "This looks like fun," her mother or father said at each stop. Somewhere along the way Jenny began to realize that maybe she was having fun after all, and she decided to stay.

Four years later Jenny, now a member of the Cherokee tribe, celebrated her fourteenth birthday at camp, making her barely eligible to be tapped out for the Indian Maiden challenge. Like Little Chief for the boys, the Indian Maiden challenge identified those girls whose camp experience, behavior, and leadership established them as candidates. The ordeal was similar to the Little Chief ordeal: a brisk late-night hike from the main campus up to the Mountain Campus, building a fire and keeping it burning, then working around camp the following day. Silence throughout the time of testing. Jenny was surprised to be selected, because she was still shy and didn't consider herself a leader. And she always declined physical challenges. "Want me to climb that high rock wall?" she would ask. "No thanks. I'll sit here and cheer my friends." Through the Indian Maiden experience, she would discover traits about herself that would change her life.

The girls were sitting silently around council ring as the names were called. Jenny heard hers, and she was shocked. A couple of days earlier, before her birthday, she wouldn't even have been eligible. But she stood where she was told and awaited her instructions. The Indian Maiden charge was read, then the entire girls' camp prayed for those who had been tapped for the challenge. After that, Jenny and the others were led into the dark.

Through the night they ran all the way to Frost Chapel and beyond. Jenny had never run a mile in her life, and she prayed every step, "God, be with me. God, be with me."

Somehow, her body was responding. She liked it. All she had wanted was make it to the campout area, and now she liked it.

Jenny arrived and built a satisfactory shelter with a tarp, sticks, and twine, but she didn't expect to need it. She knew the fire would put her out of the test—she had never built a fire in her life. She and the others were given half an hour to gather sticks, and Jenny built a small stick teepee. She received a single match, lit the little pile, and watched in amazement as the flame grew. It continued to burn for the prescribed amount of time, and she continued on through the ordeal. She slept for a few hours under her shelter, and the next day was taken back to camp, where she and the other girls who had remained a part of the challenge, worked around camp.

At the end of the day she was introduced to the other campers as an Indian Maiden. Instantly, she was a celebrity, walking with new confidence in herself and her abilities and a new trust in God to lead her through life's ordeals. That fall she joined the cross-country team at school and took on new leadership positions. She returned to WinShape for two more years as a camper, then joined our staff for four years.

Today Jenny works through Young Life to help other young people discover the talents God has given them.

Why We Do What We Do

Because of the influences of my school teachers, Sunday school teachers, coaches, and camp counselors growing up, I have spent my entire career striving to provide the same kind of inspiration. I have aimed to provide similar experiences for the young people I have encountered over the years. After watching my own children grow up, have careers, get married, and have children of their own, I realized parents need help. It takes not only parents, but also a community of people to raise children in the proper way.

I have always wanted WinShape Camps to be considered a resource that a family could rely on to help with the child development process. I experienced a harsh reality of life during the last days of my dad's life and eventual funeral in October 2006. I realized that my children learned more about their grandfather from the obituary than they actually learned from him. It was then I decided this was not going to to happen with me and my grandchildren. For this primary reason, I closed my career with WinShape after twenty-two years when I retired in May 2007.

There is just no way I can really express my appreciation to the Cathy family for allowing me to have this opportunity over the years. My appreciation goes to all of my co-workers, Chick-fil-A resource people, summer staff members, campers, and camper families who have joined me over the years to help WinShape Camps reach their current level of success.

I want to close A History of Leaders in the Making by sharing an excerpt from a scholarship reference letter that we received recently. It was written by a former camper's parent on behalf of another family's children. At the time we received the letter we thought we had only enough scholarship money to give both children half-scholarships. We learned from this letter that even that amount would not be enough.

> When I was asked to fill out David's form, I asked the mother if her older son, Chris, was going back to camp this year. She told me that her family had discussed the possibility of sending both of their sons, because Chris wanted to try to make Little Chief, and David wanted to come for the first year. She told me that they just couldn't do it, even with the scholarships that were being offered. She added that Chris is willing to sacrifice so his brother could experience Camp WinShape for the first time.
>
> I am requesting that consideration be made for both boys this summer. I know first hand how valuable the Camp WinShape experience is, as my sons attended during the first five years of its existence. One is now a presidential Secret Service agent, and the other is a U.S. Marine

captain, having served two tours of duty in Iraq. I believe that the WinShape experience helped to mold and influence their lives in a positive and enriching way so many years ago!

Reading the letter, I realized the powerful impact camp had made on the older boy, who was willing to give up his chance to become a Little Chief so his brother could experience WinShape for the first time. This, to me, is the embodiment of Truett Cathy's "I Am Third" philosophy of putting God first, others second, and yourself third.

In the end, we found the additional money and both boys were able to attend camp, and we all were blessed by the experience. This is an example of just two leaders in the making.